THE COMPLETE BOOK OF AUNTS

THE COMPLETE BOOK OF AUNTS

RUPERT CHRISTIANSEN
with Beth Brophy

Illustrated by Stephanie von Reiswitz

TWELVE

NEW YORK BOSTON

Used with permission: (16) French fashion designer Coco Chanel. Collection: Time & Life Pictures. Photographer: Roland Schoor; (17) Photo of Hillside Home School, S.001 in *The Architecture of Frank Lloyd Wright, a complete catalog, 3rd ed.* by William Allin Storrer © 2002; (19) Marcel Proust. Hulton Archive. Artist: Hulton Archive; (20) Truman Capote and his aunt Mary Ida Faulk Carter. Photo by Jennings Faulk Carter. Courtesy of Jennings Faulk Carter Collection, Monroe County Heritage Museum, Monroeville, AL; (83) Gustav Klimt's *Portrait of Adele Bloch-Bauer I*, courtesy of Getty Images; (106) Aunt Jemima portrayer Anna Robinson. Photographed between 1933 and 1951. Copyright Bettmann/CORBIS; (111) *The Andy Griffith Show*, Andy Griffith, Frances Bavier, 1960–1968 © Everett Collection/New York; (124) Rosalind Russell in *Auntie Mame*. Collection: Hulton Archive. Photographer: Hulton Archive; (169) © Peter Lofts Photography/National Portrait Gallery, London. Virginia Woolf (née Stephen) and Angelica Garnett (née Bell), by Ramsey & Muspratt. Bromide print, 1932, 7 3/4 in. x 6 3/8 in. (197 mm x 162 mm). Given by the daughter of Lettice Ramsey, Jane Burch, 1988; (185) No Place Like Home, Collection: Hulton Archive, Photographer: MGM Studios; (192) SPIDER-MAN 2, Tobey Maguire, Rosemary Harris, 2004 © Columbia/courtesy Everett Collection; (205) Dr. Ruth Westheimer, portrait, 1990 © Everett Collection/New York.

Permission for the scrapbook illustration on page 30 was granted by Rosanna Devereux.

Twelve
Hachette Book Group USA
237 Park Avenue
New York, NY 10017

Visit our Web site at www.HachetteBookGroupUSA.com.

Twelve is an imprint of Grand Central Publishing.
The Twelve name and logo is a trademark of Hachette Book Group USA, Inc.

Printed in the United States of America

First Edition: November 2007
10 9 8 7 6 5 4 3 2 1

Library of Congress Cataloging-in-Publication Data

Christiansen, Rupert
The complete book of aunts / Rupert Christiansen with Beth Brophy.—1st ed.
p. cm.
"Whether nice or nasty, bossy, timid, disappointed or eccentric, an aunt offers her brood of nieces and nephews another angle on the world and another insight into it."—Provided by the publisher.
ISBN-13: 978-0-446-58074-8
ISBN-10: 0-446-58074-0
1. Aunts—Anecdotes. 2. Aunts in literature. 3. Aunts—Family relationships. I. Brophy, Beth. II. Title.
HQ759.94.C48 2007
306.87—dc22

2007001730

Book design and text composition by L&G McRee
Illustrations by Stephanie von Reiswitz

For my sister Anna,
and in memory of J.M.M. and K.G.C.

CONTENTS

THE COMPLETE BOOK OF AUNTS

1

A SHORT HISTORY OF THE AUNT

"Why are there aunts?" asked a baffled four-year-old boy as I sat in his parents' dining room talking about this book over lunch. It's a question I cannot answer. Aunts are not ordained by nature; they do not exist in the animal world. (Elephant herds are matriarchal, and when the males are out of the way, the females band together to look after one another and nurture the calves, even to the point of adopting any orphans. But these ladies are not necessarily blood-related—they are simply public-spirited.)

Anthropologists studying kinship patterns have had little to say about aunts. Not all societies recognize them—or at least, not all languages have bothered to develop a single word to describe a mother's or father's sister: Romany has only *sachi calli*, "female relation." A separate word for "aunt" is almost nonexistent in the languages of sub-Saharan Africa, while in the extinct tongues of Old High German and Anglo-Saxon, the words *nevo* and *nift*, from which our "nephew" and "niece" are derived, appear to have been used to describe uncle and aunt and grandson and granddaughter as well. Other peoples make careful distinctions between maternal and paternal aunts, in the interests of keeping lines, laws, and customs of inheritance clearly defined. In Hindustani, for example, a paternal aunt is *phu-phi*, a maternal aunt *kala;* Latin has *matertera* and *amita;* and Scandinavian languages double up *tante* or *tant* with *faster* and *moster*.

In *The Development of Family and Marriage in Europe*, Professor Jack Goody writes, "A kinship terminology that grouped together the siblings of both parents, placing each in the same category of 'uncle' and 'aunt' (though the holders of these roles were not inter-changeable in all areas of activity) developed first in Vernacular Latin in the late Roman Empire, then spread through the Romance languages, reaching England with the Norman Conquest." But in English *aunt*, like *cousin*, continues to have a more general application as well: An aunt is not just the sister of one of your parents but any older woman with whom you are on friendly terms—an "auntie." It is in this latter sense that the aunt makes one of her rare appearances in the writings of William Shakespeare, when Puck boasts about his antics:

> The wisest aunt, telling the saddest tale,
> Sometimes for three-foot stool mistaketh me:
> Then I slip from her bum, down topples she
>
> *A Midsummer Night's Dream*, II.i

Where to begin? The Bible is uninterested in aunts; Homer and the Greek tragedians pretty much ignore them. The first aunt of any historical significance appears in ancient Rome. When Nero was three, his father, Domitius, died. Much to the fury of his atrocious mother, Agrippina, who was exiled in disgrace, the boy was sent to live with his father's aunt Domitia Lepida. Being far from respectable, she proved a thoroughly bad influence, "choosing a dancer and a barber to be his tutors," according to Suetonius.

When Claudius became emperor in 41 CE, both Nero and Agrippina were brought back to court. Agrippina loathed Domitia Lepida and instigated a campaign of vilification against her, charging her with witchcraft. "In beauty, age and wealth," writes Tacitus,

> there was little between them. Moreover, both were immoral, disreputable and violent, so they were as keen rivals in vice as in the gifts of fortune. But their sharpest issue was whether aunt or mother should stand first with

> Nero. Lepida sought to seduce his youthful character by kind words and indulgence. Agrippina, on the other hand, employed severity and menaces—she could give her son the Empire, but not endure him as Emperor. . . .

When Nero became emperor in 54 CE, he murdered Agrippina (thwarted incestuous passion being one putative motive) and then set about getting rid of Domitia Lepida, too, hoping to inherit her fortune since she was childless. "He found her confined to bed with severe constipation," Suetonius gossips:

> The old lady stroked his downy beard affectionately—he was already full-grown—murmuring: "Whenever you celebrate your coming-of-age and present me this, I shall die happy." Nero turned to his courtiers and said laughingly "in that case, I must shave at once." Then he ordered the doctors to give her a laxative of fatal strength, seized her property before she was quite dead, and tore up the will so that nothing should escape him.

After this unforgettable scene, the records go very quiet on the matter of aunts for seventeen hundred years. Whether nephews and nieces were genuinely indifferent to them we cannot know, but certainly there is little evidence of any intense emotional relationships. Uncles fare no better. For some reason, this seems to change in mid-eighteenth-century England, when aunts become the objects of affection and gratitude. We hear about Catherine Perkins, who helped her nephew William Hutton become a bookseller, and the historian Edward Gibbon's devotion to his aunt Kitty (see page 45), while novels by Samuel Richardson and Fanny Burney paint vivid pictures of their heroines' aunts, who play more than passing roles in the story. In her fascinating book *Novel Relations*, Ruth Perry attempts to relate the rise of the aunt to a deep social change that took families away from a consanguine to a conjugal model, in which loyalty toward your parents and "extended" family became less important than loyalty toward your spouse and children—a phenomenon underpinned by the drive toward capitalistic independence and small businesses, with more people marrying younger and reproducing sooner.

Why should this make aunts more important? Because, Perry suggests, they were implicated in the question—urgently asked by young women especially—of the extent to which parents should be obeyed in the quest to marry, and in the search for other adult figures who might support rebellion. This is certainly an obsessive interest of novels of the period, which repeatedly explore the theme of a girl fighting to marry the man she loves against the will of her tyrannical or uncomprehending parents—an issue made more urgent by England's Marriage Act of 1753, which made it illegal for anyone under twenty-one to marry without parental consent. Whom could a girl turn to for sympathetic, disinterested adult advice? Not a similarly inexperienced girlfriend but a wise old aunt with no ax to grind. Elizabeth Bennett's reliance on her companionable aunt Gardiner in Jane Austen's *Pride and Prejudice* is only one example.

But this is only a theory, and a rather porous, tendentious one at that. Maybe it's better just to accept that suddenly, it was time for aunthood to get its due. In the course of the next century or so, the familiar stereotypes emerge. The poet William Wordsworth's sister Dorothy is an early instance of the childless spinster aunt who grows up devoted to her big brother and then duplicates that love toward his offspring, in whose nurturing she plays a crucial role. Dorothy's particular care was the firstborn, John, born with a "noble forehead" that gave promise of a fine intellect. Alas, as Dorothy was forced to admit after attempting to homeschool him, he turned out dim and obtuse. This made no difference to her love for him. She sewed him new suits and shirts when he went off to boarding school and prayed that "God grant he may preserve his ingenuous dispositions." Finally, he got into Cambridge, where he struggled to keep up. Appointed to a curacy in the wilds of Leicestershire, he begged his aunt to come and help him settle in. So she set off, canceling an exciting holiday in Rome without a murmur of complaint.

"Nephews and nieces, whilst young and innocent, are as good almost as sons and daughters to a fervid and loving heart that has carried them in her arms from the hour they were born," writes Thomas de Quincey in his memoirs, presumably thinking of his friend Dorothy's poignant devotion to the hopeless John. "But after a nephew has grown into a huge bulk of a man, six foot high, and as stout as a bullock . . . there is nothing in such a subject to rouse the flagging pulses of the heart and to sustain a fervid spirit." Yet Dorothy was a loyal soul, and aunts can sustain their love on very little return: To be needed was sufficient joy.

The Victorian era was perhaps the aunt's finest hour, and the chapters that follow will detail several of their triumphs. Aunts (and this includes great-aunts) in the nineteenth century could be heroic figures, women who had avoided the surrender of marriage and sought spheres of activity beyond the roles of wife and mother. But chiefly they were objects of indulgent affection, in a culture that sentimentalized the relics and recollections of childhood. E. M. Forster, for instance, wrote *Marianne Thornton*, a touching memoir in tribute to his great-aunt, a woman selflessly devoted to the cause of education, who had died when he was barely seven. She had pampered and adored her little nephew, who at the time found her billing and cooing cloying and irritating. "I was in the power of a failing old woman, who wanted to be kind but she was old and each visit she was older. How old was she? 'Born in the reign of George the Fourth' my mother thought. 'More likely Edward the Fourth' cried I." When she died, she left Forster eight thousand pounds—a sum that he described as "the financial salvation of my life . . . she and no one else made my career as a writer possible." The biography, his final book, was a pious attempt to repay a debt of love and gratitude.

Aunts also become ripe for some good-natured ribbing. From the mid–nineteenth century date such innocent expletives as *my aunt!* or *my sainted aunt!* (The expression of incredulity *my aunt Fanny!* comes much later, according to the *Oxford English Dictionary*.) Aunt Sally was a fairground game, still popular in Oxfordshire pub gardens today, in which the dummy of a woman's head with a pipe sticking out of its mouth is assailed by sticks or balls aimed at dislodging the pipe—from which presumably springs the figurative use of *Aunt Sally* to

describe a person or phenomenon that is a sitting duck for criticism or mockery. An *Aunt Emma*, in the quintessential Victorian recreation of croquet, is a player who obstreperously avoids risk and aims solely to impede the progress of others.

Late in the nineteenth century and into the early twentieth, aunts seem to have become even more emphatically comic figures—some of them merely amiably dotty, such as Aunt Etty in Gwen Raverat's *Period Piece* (see page 132); some of them figures of ludicrous self-importance and rigid propriety, such as Oscar Wilde's Lady Bracknell (page 131) or P. G. Wodehouse's Aunt Agatha (page 126). The prim maiden aunt and the stingy old aunt became staple figures of theatrical farce and children's books, where they regularly make unseasonable appearances and unreasonable demands and usually soften up in the end. Uncles, it should be noted, have much less force as either figures of authority or butts of satire. In fact, uncles won't come into this book much at all, partly because so many notable aunts were unmarried.

After the Second World War, people began to tire of their aunts, identifying them with a discredited order of moral values and ramrod behavior—a force of conservatism in an age desperate to break free of the catastrophic recent past. The BBC was sneerily nicknamed Auntie, in reference to its role as guardian of public decency, while in 1953, an essay by the West End playwright Terence Rattigan conjured up the figure of Aunt Edna as the embodiment of a certain sort of theatergoer who enjoyed a Shaftesbury Avenue matinee—"a nice, respectable, middle-class middle aged maiden lady with time on her hands" who "does not appreciate Kafka" and is "in short, a hopeless lowbrow."

At the beginning of a new millennium, the great age of the aunt is over, at least in the Western world. It lasted for about two hundred years, between the mid–eighteenth century and the mid-twentieth, greatly enriching our sense of family. Aunts continue to exist biologically, of course, but they have less potency in today's society. Younger women no longer want to be called *aunt,* with its stigma of prim middle age—which is just as well, since today's children are even more distinctly disinclined to use such an uncool word. For their part, children look to idiotic celebrities rather than their elder relations for their role models. The freedoms they have and their increased access to a wide range of experience via the media mean that aunts can offer them less in the way of novelty and adventure.

In China, a nation whose citizens are encouraged to have no more than one baby, and where male children are almost superstitiously favored over female, the aunt must be classified as an endangered species. In Muslim and Hindu societies, where women have more definitely circumscribed territory and where the family remains a more cohesive institution and a more active shaper of lives than it does in Christian societies, she has a better chance of flourishing in her traditional functions and identity.

Quite what aunthood can mean among fundamentalist Christian West Africans, one cannot imagine: Recent cases of horrific child abuse reported in London saw aunts from this background involved in the unspeakably vile torturing and eventual murder of nieces they deemed to be possessed of devils in need of exorcism. *Savagery* is too mild a word.

A more edifying development in aunthood comes from the further reaches of medical technology, where it is now possible, thanks to egg donation, for a child to have his biological aunt as his biological mother, too. Emma Davies's moving account of being the aunt to her son appears on page 23. Another remarkable case of this scientific legerdemain was reported in the British press in November 2005, when thirty-two-year-old Alex Patrick, left infertile as a result of cervical cancer, won the legal right to be recognized as the mother of a baby son who was the product of her husband's sperm fertilizing her twin sister's ovum, which was then carried through pregnancy by her elder sister. It was impossible not to be moved by this remarkable instance of unselfish sisterly solidarity, itself a bedrock of aunthood and the familial affections that fill this book.

ETYMOLOGICAL AUNTS

Most European languages use a one- or two-syllable word that appears to have derived from the ancient Greek *tethis* or the Latin *amita* and *tata*. The latter—a word meaning "rearer"—could be assigned to a father or a wet nurse as well as an aunt.

Czech, Croatian: *teta*
French, Dutch, German: *tante*
Finnish: *tati*
Italian: *Zia*
Russian: *tetya*
Spanish, Portuguese: *tia*
Turkish: *teyze*

Farther afield, "aunt" is otherwise rendered:

Basque: *izeba*
Guarany: *sy'y*
Hungarian: *nagyneni*
Kikuyu: *taata*
Sanskrit: *nanandaa*
Swahili: *shagazi*
Welsh: *modryb*

Japanese: *amitam* (rather alarmingly, the word for "mother's sister" is the same as that for "father's concubine")

According to the *Oxford English Dictionary*, the word *aunt* first appears in written English around 1300, derived from the Old French *aunte* or *ante*. This usage survives today in the way that children are enjoined to call close but unrelated female family friends Aunt or Auntie. In the more louche periods of the seventeenth century, the word briefly entered smart urban slang as a term for "prostitute," "procuress," or "brothel-keeper."

In sign language, "aunt" is indicated by clenching the right hand and leaving the thumb facing upward to form the letter *A*, then holding the hand close to your right cheek and shaking it slightly back and forth.

An oddity of French: *Tante* is also a popular heterosexual term of abuse for a homosexual—the equivalent of "nancy-boy" or "pansy."

An oddity of English: Although *uncle* has been comfortably related to *avuncular* since the 1830s, no equivalent adjective has ever evolved from *aunt*. In this book, I am resorting to *auntly*, a word that, according to the *OED*, had only a brief and feeble currency: In 1844, Lady Lyttelton's letters send "my best regards and Auntly blessings to my nephew," and two years later Sara Coleridge's memoirs record "a very motherly and auntly tale." But it never caught on—why?

THE AUNT HEAP

This term is said to be Prince Charles's satirical nickname for Kensington Palace, in reference to its warren of grace-and-favor apartments, occupied by his elderly female relations.

COCO CHANEL (1883-1971)

The French couturier considered by many to be the single most influential arbiter of fashion in the twentieth century could owe it all to her aunts. Gabrielle Bonheur Chanel, nicknamed Coco (for "little pet"), was orphaned at age six. She was raised in Auvergne by two aunts, who taught her to sew. Had it not been for those early sewing lessons, Chanel might have wound up in another line of work.

In 1922, she introduced her Chanel No. 5 perfume.

In 1952, Chanel designed her signature cardigan jacket.

Her signature quilted handbag with the chain-link strap is still popular today and retails for fifteen hundred dollars and up, depending on the size and type of leather.

At the time of her death in 1971, Chanel was still working. Since 1983, Karl Lagerfeld has been chief designer of her fashion house, and has been instrumental in updating the classic Chanel looks into modern clothing and accessories for today's chic and wealthy fashion trendsetters.

Coco Chanel

FRANK LLOYD WRIGHT (1867-1959)

The first commissioned work of another great and influential icon of the twentieth century, the architect Frank Lloyd Wright, is connected to his aunts Jane and Nell Lloyd-Jones, who in 1886 founded the Hillside Home School, a coed boarding school near Spring Green, Wisconsin. Wright's first commissioned work was to design some buildings and a windmill for the school. After the facility closed in 1915, Wright pursued the idea of repairing the damaged buildings and incorporating them into an institution devoted to the study and practice of architecture. The first twenty-three apprentices formed the Taliesin Fellowship in 1932. The Taliesin estate, Wright's Wisconsin home, became a National Historic Landmark in 1976.

FAMOUS WRITERS AND THEIR AUNTS

Leo Tolstoy (1828-1910)

Many consider the author of *War and Peace* and *Anna Karenina* to be the greatest of all novelists. He was born into a noble family, and after his parents died—his mother when he was two, his father when he was nine—Tolstoy was raised by several relations, among them his aunt the Countess Pelageya Yushkova and the distant kinswoman Tatyana Aleksandrovna Yergolskaya. He called the latter Tante Toinette and later claimed that she had "had the greatest influence on my life," inasmuch as she had taught him "the moral joy of love."

Marcel Proust (1871-1922)

> The taste was that of the little piece of madeleine, which on Sunday mornings at Combray (because on those mornings I did not go out before Mass), when I went to say good morning to her in her bedroom, my Aunt Léonie used to give me, dipping it first in her own cup of tea or tisane.

This key scene in Proust's vast novel *Remembrance of Things Past* (*A la recherche du temps perdu*) shows the adult narrator

Marcel Proust

discovering that the taste and smell of his aunt's madeleine cookie, a familiar feature of his childhood, releases a flood of vivid memories.

Truman Capote (1924-1984)

This photo of Truman Capote and his aunt Mary Ida Faulk Carter was shot during a visit by Capote to his childhood home in Monroeville in April 1963 while he was working on *In Cold Blood*.

Born in New Orleans, Truman Capote was abandoned by his teenage mother and for some years lived with his elderly aunts in Monroeville, Alabama. Although he is best known for *In Cold Blood*, he also wrote a fictionalized memoir of this period called "A Christmas Memory." One of these aunts, Marie Rudisill, later felt compelled to write her own version, titled *Truman Capote: The Story of His Bizarre and Exotic Boyhood by an Aunt Who Helped Raise Him*. Later, she won another sort of fame when she appeared as "the Fruitcake Lady" on *The Tonight Show*.

F. Scott Fitzgerald (1896-1940)

The young Fitzgerald very much wanted to go to Princeton, but there was doubt as to whether his family—once well-off but now impoverished—could afford to send him. His maiden aunt Annabel McQuillan offered to pay for his college education at Georgetown University, a Catholic school, but Fitzgerald was not interested. Paying for his tuition at Princeton was solved by the death of his grandmother, who left his mother a sum of money.

2
MOTHERING AUNTS

TWENTY-FIRST CENTURY AUNT

Over the past few decades, scientific advances have led to an amazing feat in the history of aunthood: women, such as Emma Davies, who can be both mother and aunt to the same child. Here Davies discusses the birth of her nephew and son Seth:

Seth is my nephew: His mother is my sister, and his father is my brother-in-law. Seth's conception took place in a clinic petri dish; the sperm was my brother-in-law's, and the egg was mine. He looks very much like his father and shares his dashing eccentric style in clothes and sense of humor. Nevertheless he reminds us all of my son Peter when he was Seth's age.

My sister Flora asked me to give her an egg and I was pleased she did. She and my brother-in-law Hugh had experienced eight years of disappointment, which culminated in the devastating stillbirth of their naturally conceived daughter. By the time Flora and I had our first conversation about egg donation, Mark, my husband, and I considered every way we might help them get a baby, including having one and giving it to them. Now that we had heard about egg donation, it seemed a very simple and natural thing to do for my sister, who in a great many ways had brought me up since I was fifteen.

Until I was fifteen I lived in the shadow of my sister's brilliant, rebellious school career and her powerful presence at home. Flora took my education in hand; she gave me a copy of The Female Eunuch, *introduced me to her radical friends, and encouraged me in my sexual adventures. When our father died, we curled up in a bed together and slept through the wretched afternoon. After Dad's death, we spent a long time together going over and over our parents' unhappy marriage and how it had affected us. I turned out to be a lackadaisical feminist; although committed in spirit, I was lazy. I slept through university lectures and arrived in London with no degree or clue as to how I was to earn my living. By contrast, Flora was working hard as a criminal defense lawyer. Never without a man in her life, she swore she would never have children and certainly never get married. When I rang to tell her I was going to have a baby, her comment was, "I expect you're going to make a career of this." She was and is a fabulous aunt, and our sons are extremely close to her and Hugh.*

If I, Mark, Flora, and Hugh had not remained so close through their long efforts to get pregnant, especially during their pregnancy and its terrible end with the prenatal death of their baby girl Dora, Seth's story might have been less straightforward. As it was, none of us could think of any reason to give the psychologist at the clinic as to why we shouldn't do it. Quite soon after we'd all agreed to give egg donation a try, Flora and Hugh looked into adoption and were given a three-month-old girl, Melody, to be their daughter. Her arrival was momentous and we were all ravished by her. The ghastliness of the death of Dora, Flora and Hugh's baby, and the awful years of unsuccessful fertility treatment were over; somehow Melody made sense of it all. Flora and Hugh's adoration of her was marvelous to see, and they took to the nurturing of Melody with easy confidence and joy. When not long after Melody's arrival Flora suggested that we go ahead with the egg donation, I reacted powerfully against it. Instead of feeling excited about the process, as I had previously, it became unreasonably menacing. I found the prospect of the physical intrusion threatening, whereas before it had been insignificant. Also, I became intractable over dates. It must have seemed very peculiar as I hadn't really got much to do except a show of my paintings that was coming up. I had always been cavalier about my health, consuming anything going. I think I behaved like this because it was too soon to revisit the traumas that Melody had put behind us, but I didn't quite realize it at the time.

It was a good thing to have delayed it, for we all agreed later that Melody's place in the world would certainly have been undermined had Flora fallen pregnant shortly after Melody's arrival. Flora and Hugh accepted my contrariness with great understanding; they didn't mention eggs again until Melody became such an integral part of all our lives that we could barely remember life without her. This time the atmosphere was different; Flora and Hugh had Melody, we agreed we were going to attempt one cycle to produce this baby, and all desperation disappeared. It was exciting. Our visits to the psychologist and the clinic were made in this spirit. There was a sense of unreality about it: I don't think any of us believed, or dared hope, it would result in a baby. Besides which, the doctors made us feel as though we were part of an experiment in eugenics and gave us frightful giggles.

Though I hate needles, Mark got so good at giving me injections in my bottom, I didn't mind. The clinic made a mistake and overstimulated my ovaries, and then wanted to scrap the procedure. I felt furious with them, as it seemed to prove their lack of humane interest in our case. It would have been very dispiriting for everyone to have to begin again, so we insisted on carrying on. The day of the beginning of Seth's conception was bizarre and very moving. As I staggered down the corridor to the room where the eggs were to be harvested (because of their miscalculation, I had so many in my ovaries it was uncomfortable to walk or sit up), I turned back to wave at Flora in the hall and to Hugh, who was climbing the stairs, with great dignity, to the room where he was to produce the sperm.

Three days later, three fertilized eggs were placed in Flora's womb; five others were put in a deep freeze. Flora's pregnancy had the same wonder about it as the Virgin Mary's—except, unlike Mary, we never got over our disbelief, even when we looked at the scan and could clearly see a boy. The closer it came to Seth's birth, the more incredible it became. Waiting at the hospital on the day of Seth's birth, while Flora and Hugh were in the operating room (it was a cesarean section to minimize risk, so I was not allowed to be with them), was an agony of anxiety. I had sat with them during the stillbirth of Dora in the same hospital and was fully expecting to go through the same experience. I think we all were. It was impossible to separate the happiness from relief when Hugh finally appeared to tell me that Seth and Flora were safe and well.

Today our family has just gotten back from Seth's fourth birthday party. Flora had cooked a delicious tea for Seth and his guests. Flora and Hugh made the party fun, warm, and hospitable for us all, and everyone, especially Seth, surrounded by his friends and lovingly presided over by Melody, who is now six, had a lovely time.

When Flora approached the clinic to carry out the donation, the consultant was anxious about our being siblings. For me, it has made it beautifully simple: We share the same genetic pool. The way Flora does things is familiar—her cooking (which we both assimilated from our mother), the chaos we share in our separate houses, ideas about a good day out—and I know her great sense of humor, her outspokenness, her great pleasure in things. Both Mark and I love Hugh very much and admire and respect him, not least for the incredible support he gave Flora in her pursuit of children. (Hugh had mumps when he was nineteen and so wasn't figuring to have any children.) If I had any doubt that Seth and Melody were not being so fully loved and cared for in every way, I should be overwrought by it, and in Seth's case resentful and angry. But I was convinced that with Flora and Hugh, this scenario would never happen. I am aware, too, that if I didn't love and respect Hugh, I would have felt anxious about entering into our new relationship and then the joy of its success might be awkward.

Flora and I have survived a quarrel since then—and not a polite one, either, but a real fight in the style of our childhood, Flora torpedoing me with well-aimed missiles and then it ending up with me throwing her a punch. It was a bit shocking for everyone—especially Mark and Hugh, who had not witnessed us in our childhood roles before. We got over it, though.

I don't feel any more maternal for Seth than I do for Melody, but when I am with him I do feel very happy that I could help in his beginnings. While Flora was pregnant, the four of us had a conversation about whether Seth's biological mother should be an open issue, or whether it would contravene a basic right for Seth to be able to choose whether he wants his origins to be out in the open. It has become an open subject and it would have been strange had it been otherwise, as it is a house without taboos. Still, after Seth was born and for his first couple of years, I stood back a little more than I might have had I not thought there was a danger of Flora feeling I was hovering about too much. Now Melody and Seth often come over to our house and spend the day with us, and we spend weekends at their house in the country. One day, when I was driving them over to my house, Melody said from the back, "Emma, you know, Seth and I both have two mothers. I have my mother and Flora is my mother and Seth has you and Flora is his mother, too." It was said with absolute certainty and without a trace of confusion. I looked around and Seth was nodding and grinning.

GREAT MOTHERING AUNTS IN HISTORY

Lennon's Mimi: All You Need Is Love

Liverpool, 1940. Julia Stanley's marriage to the feckless Alf Lennon dismayed her respectable middle-class family. When Julia gave birth to a baby boy, her younger sister Mimi went to see the child in the hospital and felt immediately that she was destined "to be his mother." She chose the name *John* for him, with Julia patriotically adding *Winston* to the moniker.

Five years later, when Alf had drifted off and Julia had taken up with another man, Mimi insisted that she should take control of John and give him the proper stable family upbringing that Julia was unable to provide. Julia meekly accepted, and John moved to Mendips, a semidetached house in a pleasant Protestant suburb of Liverpool. The mayor lived next door.

Mimi had trained as a nurse and then become a secretary. In 1939, she had married George Smith, a quiet, amiable dairy farmer. They were very happy together, as far as anyone knows, but because she had spent so much of her childhood looking after her three younger sisters, Mimi let it be known that she did not want children of her own. Psychologists may see the appropriation of her sister's son in terms of displacement and surrogacy, but the simple fact is that Mimi loved John with a true enduring love that never faltered or softened or lied. "I would sometimes rant and rave at him, but deep down he knew I loved him and that he loved me," she said. "We were very close." Love, love, love, all you need is love—and John Lennon was given plenty of it.

But it must have been confusing for the boy, being pulled in so many emotional directions. If strangers in the street took him for Mimi's son, she would not contradict them, yet he would also privately ask her, "Why can't I call you mummy?" He adored his uncle George, but his biological father had effectively vanished. Meanwhile, in a strange inversion of nature, Julia became in effect his aunt, visiting regularly, sometimes daily, and lavishing him with indulgent affection and treats. Her second relationship produced two girls, John's half sisters. None of this was clearly discussed or explained, and however anchored he was on his Mimi mummy (the assonance itself causing a further puzzle), John was consequently prey to a jumble of conflicting relationships and confusing presences and absences. The result was an anxious, anarchic, aggressive, ambitious, selfish, softhearted, crazy, mixed-up kid who led the local posse and fought and stole and swore and rode the bumpers of the tramcars when Mimi wasn't looking. He could well have turned delinquent, and nearly did.

Within the walls of Mendips, however, things moved serenely, and he was happy. Mimi was a conventional disciplinarian, emphasizing the value of domestic routine, cleanliness, and good manners. She gave up work to rear John, and proudly claimed that "he never came back to an empty house." He was required to mow the lawn, clean his room, and go to church on Sundays. His pocket money was five bob; entertainment was limited to a trip to the pantomime at Christmas and the latest Walt Disney movie in the summer. Most significantly, it was a house with plenty of good books: John was consumed by *Just William, The Wind in the Willows*, and *Alice's Adventures in Wonderland*, and from the age of seven he began producing his own volumes of skits, cartoons, and stories.

"My husband and I gave him a wonderful home," Mimi claimed later, with justification. "I never forgave my auntie for not treating me like a genius," he later complained, only half joking. But she always knew that he would "amount to something," and he should have given her credit for providing the secure and comfortable environment from which he could mount a creative rebellion that would make him, fifteen years later, as famous as anyone on the planet.

Clearly a bright boy, he earned his place at one of the best local grammar schools, Quarry Bank—a sensible, conservative institution that might have turned him into a doctor or a lawyer. Instead it unwittingly fed a nasty little so-and-so, the class comedian, lying and swearing and talking back to the masters. "I was aggressive because I wanted to be popular," he told the Beatles' biographer Hunter Davies later. "I wanted everybody to do what I told them to do, to laugh at my jokes and let me be the boss." Liberal application of the cane proved no deterrent, and Mimi came to dread the telephone ringing at home during the day: The caller was usually the headmaster, complaining about the boy's latest misdemeanor. Having been ranked at the top of the first form, John ended up failing all his O-levels.

Music began to dominate John's imagination. Mimi had delighted in his wild drawings and verbal inventiveness, and it was this creative streak that she attempted to encourage. But Uncle George had started something when he slipped the boy his first musical instrument, an old mouth organ, which he played incessantly. Mimi did not much like music and deplored what she considered a rubbishy noise, but his mother played the banjo, bought him a cheap ten-pound guitar, and taught him some basic chords.

Mimi made him practice them out on the front porch. Later

she relented to the extent of buying him a superior fourteen-pound guitar, but she remained skeptical about his talent. "Stick to art," she told him in what would become one of the most celebrated remarks in the Beatles mythology. "The guitar's all right as a hobby, John, but you'll never make a living with it."

It was the mid-1950s—an era in which the teenager, wriggling free of postwar deprivation and puritanism, became the new social force, disruptive and disloyal. It was the era of rock 'n' roll, when popular music became pop and dance floors turned Dionysian to the tunes of Bill Haley and His Comets, Buddy Holly and the Crickets, and the sensual power of Elvis Presley. Infatuated with their vitality, John Lennon and some of his school friends set up a crude folk music band called the Quarrymen. One Saturday afternoon in 1956, they were playing at a church fete. Someone brought along a boy from the other side of the tracks—of whom Mimi, with her innocently snobbish insistence on respectability and the proprieties of caste, could never quite approve. His name was Paul McCartney, and what happened next belongs elsewhere in the story.

Throughout the years of John's delinquency, Mimi staunchly held the fort at Mendips. There were tragedies, which the boy in his self-centered adolescent innocence never fully confronted—Uncle George dying suddenly, his mother being killed in a car accident. Mimi's values remained immovable. She refused to countenance music as his destiny, made the plebeian Paul and George Harrison unwelcome in the house, and pushed John into art college. He did no work at all there, as Mimi eventually intuited. One day she tracked him down to a dirty Liverpool dive known as the Cavern, where the band now calling itself the Beatles was playing in the lunch hour. She was appalled. "Try as I might, I just couldn't get near the stage," she recalled. "If I could, I would have pulled him off it." So she fought her way into his dressing room. "Very nice, John," she said with grim sarcasm. "This is very nice."

In desperation, she signed him up to be a bus conductor, but he was nearly twenty and ready to take the first avenue of escape—the wild port of Hamburg, where the Beatles had been offered work in a club. For the time being, she had lost the battle. But when their first Hamburg gig came to an end, John went straight back to Mendips, throwing stones against Mimi's bedroom window in the middle of the night and shouting at her to let him in. He stormed upstairs, ignoring her lecture, and lay in his bedroom for a week.

For the next two years, until the advent of Brian Epstein and the big time, Mimi continued to exert what influence she could over her errant nephew—and at some level, her opinion, or at least her presence, continued to matter to him. He moved out, but the night before his shotgun wedding to Cynthia Powell, he came back to her and broke down in tears. Cynthia was a nice middle-class Protestant girl he had known since art college days, but Mimi realized that she was not his intellectual match and refused to attend the register-office ceremony. (Later, the two women became close, staying together while the Beatles were touring.) And he persuaded her to listen to the band's first recorded single, "Love Me Do," to which her response was a characteristic harrumph. "If you think you're going to make your fortune with that, you've got another think coming."

"Remember I said I'd be famous," he retorted.

"What always worried me, John, was that you wouldn't be so much famous as notorious." They were both right.

Once John had left home for good and the world was at his feet, singing his songs and laughing at his jokes, Mimi could only be proud of him. For all the cheap contempt that became his stock-in-trade, her boy had turned out well, and journalists who beat their way past her well-scrubbed front door discovered that Mimi could be tolerant of, and even amused by, his antics. "Every time John does something bad and gets his picture in the papers, he rings me up to smooth me over. A big present arrives every time he's been naughty"—one of them being his MBE (Member of the Order of the British Empire), which he came and pinned to her breast, remarking that she deserved it more than he did. She displayed it on top of the television.

In 1965, when the fans pestering her outside Mendips had become an impossible nuisance, he bought her a bungalow in an exclusive enclave in Dorset. "I know it's stupid. But nothing could compensate for the pleasure he gave me as a boy," she told Hunter Davies when he visited her there. "He comes to see me as often as he can. He sat up on the roof for four days in the summer. I ran up and down getting drinks for him. He never shows much emotion. He finds it hard to say sorry. But one night he said that even if he didn't come down to see me every day, or every month, he always thought about me at some time every day, wherever he was. That meant a great deal to me."

When he fell under the sway of Yoko Ono and based himself in New York, John would still call Mimi every week for long conversations, during which they teased each other affectionately. "Hi, Father Christmas here," was his customary greeting. She criticized his clothes, the way he flung money around, and his mumbling incoherence, but she seems to have been unfazed by his increasingly bizarre behavior. Even his stark naked appearance alongside Yoko on the cover of their bonkers *Two Virgins* album didn't shock her—after all, she'd presumably seen everything he bared plenty of times before. "It would have been all right, John, but you're both so ugly. Why don't you get somebody attractive on the cover if you've got to have someone completely naked?" He must have thought that funny.

In the 1970s, holed up in the Dakota apartment building in New York, he became increasingly eccentric and withdrawn. Unable to return to Britain for fear of losing his American visa, his nostalgia for Liverpool became sentimental and intense, and his accent (a source of embarrassment to Mimi, who had brought him up to speak an unaccented Queen's English) more marked. He asked Mimi to send him mementos—glass and china, a grandfather clock, old postcards and photographs—remembered from Mendips. He even started to wear his old school tie, and urged Mimi to come and live in an apartment in the Dakota. Her work being done, her bones weary, she pooh-poohed the idea. "No fear, John, you'll never catch me over there. I have never liked Americans. And you shouldn't be there either, it's no good for you."

It wasn't. One morning in December 1980, two months after John's fortieth birthday, Mimi was lying in bed and heard his name mentioned when she switched on the radio. Being drowsy, she did not register the context, and only later, when a friend of John's called on her, did she hear the terrible news that her boy had been shot dead in the street by a lunatic. Stunned with grief, she cut off her hair. "I will never recover," she told the world in a statement.

In her final years, she moved back to Liverpool, dying in 1991 at the age of eighty-eight. Yoko Ono, Cynthia, and her great-nephew Sean all came to the funeral. The Beatles have become a chapter in cultural history in which Aunt Mimi's mummy role is honored, and Mendips is now owned by the National Trust, serving as an example of the postwar middle-class gentility that John Winston Lennon despised yet owed so much to.

The Brontës' Aunt Branwell

When the meek and gentle Maria Brontë died in 1821, her last words were "Oh God my poor children oh God my poor children." Six of them stood in a bleak cold parsonage, in the stony gray village of Haworth on the moors of Yorkshire, with their stubborn, self-centered, and emotionally troubled father: Maria, seven; Elizabeth, six; Charlotte, five; Branwell, four; Emily, three; and Anne, one. Over the past seven months, they had watched and heard their mother perish, in ever more excruciating pain. She might well feel anguish for their future.

To be left motherless is a universal human tragedy, drawing the aunt out of the shadows to take center stage in a bereaved family not quite her own. The role she must dutifully play is not always gratifying. She may be considered an intruder, or branded second best. She may be required to sacrifice elements of her own life, nurturing nieces and nephews without access to the biological taproot of parenthood. To those who have known the intimate romantic sweetness of maternal love, she can assuage but never altogether compensate.

The Reverend Patrick Brontë suffered from demons, and did not warm easily to his offspring. He needed another wife, but could not find one—three women he approached smartly rejected his unappealing offer. The alternative was his wife's sister, Elizabeth, who had nursed Maria in her dying days. She was over forty and had a home she liked in Cornwall, but her Methodist piety meant that she could not find a way to refuse. So Aunt Branwell—the children always called her by her surname, a customary practice until the later nineteenth century—became the substitute, contributing her inherited annual income of fifty pounds to the household and occupying a small bedroom that at first she shared with baby Anne.

She lacked charm and warmth, and never adjusted to Yorkshire ways. The servants found her "a bit of a tyke . . . so crosslike an' fault finding, and so close." Charlotte's lifelong friend Ellen Nussey remembered her more appealingly as "a very small, antiquated little lady. She wore caps large enough for half a dozen of the present fashion, and a front of light auburn curls over her forehead. She always dressed in silk."

As she grew older, the biting Yorkshire climate seems to have worn her down. She became increasingly straitlaced and reluctant to leave her bedroom, emerging only for a Sunday excursion to church, where her brother-in-law made a stern preacher. Against the wind and the damp, she kept her window bolted and the fire banked up. Meals would be taken to her on a tray, and after mornings being intellectually schooled by their father, the children would be sent up to her every afternoon to sit still and do their duty.

Yet it was the cantankerous Branwell who appears to have been her favorite—he was certainly the one who grieved most when she died, recalling her as "the guide and director of all the happy days connected with my childhood." The three girls (Elizabeth and Maria both died as a result of the appalling rigors of a local boarding school) merely bowed to her yoke. Needle and thread were the fundamental elements of her daily regime, wielded—according to another of Charlotte's friends, Mary Taylor—"with purpose or without. . . . She used to keep the girls sewing charity clothing and maintained to me that it was not for the good of the recipients but of the servers. 'It was proper for them to do it,' she said."

Aunt Branwell remained unaware of what went on when the children were alone downstairs—a secret ferment of imaginative life and the creation of the fantasy world of Gondal, which later led Charlotte and Emily to produce three of the most powerful and original novels of the century. "She was not her nieces' confidante," Patrick Brontë admitted to Charlotte's biographer Mrs. Gaskell when they discussed Aunt Branwell. But although her culture and her values were narrow, she had no instinct to interfere; as long as her rules and her routines were observed, she was not ambitious for power over her charges.

"She and her nieces went on smoothly enough," wrote Mrs. Gaskell, "and though they might now and then be annoyed by petty tyranny, she still inspired them with sincere respect, and not a little affection. They were, moreover, grateful to her for many habits she had enforced upon them, and which in time had become second nature: order, method, neatness in everything; a perfect knowledge of all kinds of household work; an exact punctuality, and obedience to the laws of time and place . . . with their impulsive natures it was positive repose to have learnt obedience to external laws."

Nor was Aunt Branwell mercenary. In 1841, when Charlotte and Emily hatched a plan to train as teachers in Belgium and then return to take over Miss Wooler's school on Dewsbury Moor, Charlotte wrote to ask her aunt for a loan. The letter certainly shows no whiff of intimidation. Indeed, given the limitation of her aunt's resources, Charlotte could be accused of a boldness bordering on arm-twisting:

> You always like to use your money to the best advantage. You are not fond of making shabby purchases; when you do confer a favor, it is often done in style; and, depend upon it, £50, or £100, thus laid out, would be well employed. Of course, I know no other friend in the world to whom I could apply on this subject, except yourself. I feel an absolute conviction that, if this advantage were allowed us, it would be the making of us for life. . . . I want us *all* to get on. I know we have talents, and I want them to be turned to account. I look to you, aunt, to help us. I think you will not refuse.

She did not refuse, and Charlotte and Emily went to Belgium. Within months, however, Aunt Branwell had died from cancer, unrewarded and maybe unthanked for her steady devotion. She was given no way in: From the moment she arrived at Haworth, Aunt Branwell would have confronted a hexagonal web of delicate relationships and loyalties, consolidated over a deathbed.

Gibbon's Kitty: Rising to the Task

It was easier for Catherine Porten. When she inherited Edward Gibbon in 1747, his six siblings had all died, and only this one frail ten-year-old, with an outsize head and spindly frame, survived. He had not been close to his mother, and following her demise he was delighted when his lugubrious and uncommunicative father sent him to live with her father and unmarried sister. Recalling Aunt Kitty in his autobiography, he felt "a tear of gratitude" trickling down his cheek. "If there are any who rejoice that I live," the historian of *The Decline and Fall of the Roman Empire* continued, "to that dear and excellent woman they must hold themselves indebted."

Unlike Aunt Branwell, Kitty was great fun, and she and the orphaned Edward shared tastes and interests. "Her indulgent tenderness, the frankness of her temper, and my innate rising curiosity soon removed all distance between us." Skeptical of ardent religion, she and the boy would engage in free moral discussion, and she introduced him to Pope's translations of Homer and the enthralling *Arabian Nights*. "To my aunt's kind lessons, I ascribe my early and invincible love of reading which I would not exchange for the treasures of India." Under such tutelage, his health improved and his deformities faded. The roles of aunt and nephew dissolved: "She was truly my mother, she became my friend."

When Edward got into some trouble over gambling debts at age eighteen, it was to her generosity that he applied for a bail-out. "I know you have thoughts of doing something for me by your will, I beg you only to anticipate it. . . . I tremble for your answer but beg it may be speedy." It is a testament to the strength of their relationship that Kitty refused the plea, and Gibbon never resented her firmness. Throughout his life, she continued to be his "dear Kitty," and he wrote to her with unfailing affection and candor. For her part, she took enormous pride in his literary achievements and lived on resiliently into her seventies, "a giddy girl . . . never out of order above four and twenty hours at a time . . . one of the youngest women I know about town."

Sadly, she died in 1786, two years before the completion of *Decline and Fall*. "A good understanding, and an excellent heart, with health, spirits and a competency; to live in the midst of her friends till the age of fourscore and then to shut her eyes without pain or remorse. Death can only have deprived her of some years of weakness, perhaps of misery," Gibbon reflected. "All this is perfectly true, but all these reflections will not dispel a thousand sad and tender remembrances." This is the simplest case of a mothering aunt—a meeting of like minds uncomplicated by any severe test of loyalties, as neither party ever married or was otherwise encumbered.

FAMILY MATTERS

Fifty-two-year-old Maile Hulihan of Sudbury, Massachusetts, on her relationship with her nephews, now nine and twelve:

It's unusual these days for extended families to be involved in each other's day-to-day lives, the way it is for me and my sister. She lives in the next town. We joke that it's good to have someone you can dump your kids on without feeling guilty.

In February 2000, my sister's family was in a horrific car accident in Florida. My brother-in-law was killed, my sister was badly injured, and my nephews, then six and three, were slightly hurt. I got on a plane, took the boys out of the hospital, and stayed in a hotel with them as my sister underwent surgery. One night the youngest woke suddenly screaming, "Daddy, Daddy."

Going to Florida wasn't a decision; it was a necessity for me to be with my sister and the kids. The kids know me the best and I wanted them to feel safe and cared for during that horrible experience, and I had to advocate for my sister's medical care.

When my sister got out of the hospital, they moved in with my family and me. My sister couldn't take care of them while she was recovering, and we were all grieving. We tried to keep their life normal after the accident. They shared a room with my son for a while. We'd give them baths every night. To get them in their pajamas, we'd have to chase them as they ran naked through the hallways.

We made a commitment to raise our families together because we wanted them to have an aunt as an outlet for whatever came up. My son is the same age as my oldest nephew. We are all close. For my husband and me, it's like we have three kids, not one, and it's the same for my sister.

I know my nephews pretty well, and they treat my house like their house, including raiding the snack drawer every time they visit. Our families have dinner every Sunday night at one of our houses and we plan and organize our week. We spend holidays together, Halloween and Thanksgiving and Christmas. We go on vacations together. Last summer both families went to Italy. It brought tears to my eyes to bring the boys to art museums and transmit my love of art and history to them.

My son is close to both of his cousins, but they are really more like siblings, including knowing how to push each other's buttons. My husband is very close to them, too. He's the sports guy who went to all their games. Recently my sister became engaged, but it's already apparent that her fiancé is joining our family life. He will blend in with us.

It's easier to ask a kid who is not your own direct questions about social lives or friends. With my nephews, I will often introduce a sensitive topic. They feel comfortable talking to me. My sister and I both teach religious instruction in our eldest sons' class at church because we want to be able to pass on our values in a way that's reinforced by each other.

Being an aunt means that I've opened my heart to them, like I do for my own child. I accept responsibility for them, I look out for them. I wasn't going to have more than one child, but now it feels like I did. I know what they're allergic to, what medications they take, and how they've done each school year. Having an intimate experience with three boys rather than one has made my life richer. It has enhanced my parental radar system. They're happy kids and I love to hear them laugh with my son.

When they reach high school, which is in my town, they'll come to my house after school. My sister is a clinical psychologist and I'm not working anymore, so it's easier for me to assume that after-school role. My husband is retired. He wants to move to a warmer climate but we've agreed to wait until the boys finish high school. We want to continue as a joint family through their teenage years, which promise to be almost as challenging as anything we've gone through so far.

3

HEROIC AUNTS

In the course of the nineteenth century, the aunt seems to have marched into history, striding through society with a spring in her step, no longer confined to her ancillary role in the family. The female sphere was expanding, turning faster. Middle-class women could begin to define themselves beyond wifedom, motherhood, spinsterhood, and dutiful philanthropy, as the narrow range of professions available to them at the beginning of the century—the stage, literature, artistic crafts, infant teaching—expanded into science, medicine, adult education, and even political agitation. Railways and steam power increased their mobility. George Sand made romantic passion if not respectable, then at least a possibility. By 1900, the great questions about women—where should she stand in relation to men, what role should she play, how far could she go—urgently required answers.

In this process, the unmarried aunt became heroic. She could be her own woman, rather than one defined by her relationship to the patriarchal family. She had her cause, her ideal, her crusade, her destiny. She had work to do, which took her out of the home and gave her dignity in the eyes of the world. Yet her aunthood bonded her with the young, rooting her in the soil of family. This gave her enough of human love; no man need set her fluttering, no batsqueak of erotic yearning seems to have troubled her existence.

FORMIDABLE TANTE ESTHÈRE

Meredith Resnick, forty-five, a freelance writer in Irvine, California, on her aunt Esther:

I didn't know the word as a child, but intimidated was what I felt around Aunt Esther.

She was a world traveler, and sometimes she'd even come all the way from Manhattan on the diesel train to stay the weekends with us in Yonkers. I knew I was supposed to love her, but she made my palms sweat.

One of the first women to graduate from the Harvard School of Public Health, she went on to work for the World Health Organization. Aunt Esther had huge lolling breasts, thick ankles, and wore sensible dresses even when the humid air hung like embroidery, like a moldy shawl on her back. It protected her image. She squeezed her wide feet into Ferragamo pumps, rarely smiled, and insisted you call her Tante Esthère, preferably with an accent de Français.

Aunt Esther was never a mother or a wife; she was a midwife who delivered other people's babies and told the husbands what to do. She was bossy. And probably, everyone said, a lesbian.

She never talked about that. Ever. But looking back, I see her biggest challenge was not the obvious—trying to fit in a culture and era that suppressed women. Her biggest challenge was just plain trying to fit in, [something] that would only come from accepting herself for who she was.

She was blessed with brains but cursed with pride. She focused, with all good intentions, on "bettering" the rest of us. I was much younger than my siblings (by twenty-one years) and new material for Aunt Esther to shape: sensitive, shy, introspective, and lacking confidence. She took me to Lincoln Center and the Guggenheim Museum; the United Nations and Central Park. I wore gloves and dresses. She showed me how to drink tea with my pinkie extended, though I never did it quite right. Her mouth tightened. "Keep practicing," she said.

Thank goodness, she started bringing me books.

I remember the first time. At the end of our living room was a green-and-white club chair. Tante Esthère sat on the wide cushion like a throne and I sat on the arm, close enough to smell the Aqua Net in her hair. She cracked open Doctor Dolittle, *pressed the cover page down with her polished index finger, took a deep breath.*

Magic.

Sentences rolled off her tongue in English, French, and Spanish. She used accents and read to me in different voices, reading over passages I liked, letting me read to her—and when I did, she didn't criticize. This was not Tante Esthère, was it? Nor was I the scared, intimidated six-year-old.

We took turns with dialogue and she showed me how to look up words in the dictionary, told me it didn't mean I wasn't smart if I had to do that. I started looking forward to her visits. We read My Friend Flicka *and* Charlie and the Chocolate Factory.

She read to me past my bedtime. Once she stayed an extra night just so we could finish a book. She owned words, and then, miraculously, I owned them, too.

I started to love her—at least when she was sitting in that green-and-white chair with a book. She seemed nicer, somehow, maybe because her own fears about who she was evaporated during those interludes. When she read to me, somehow we were both freed. Maybe that was a gift I gave my aunt as much as the one she gave me.

HEROIC AUNTS IN HISTORY

Caroline Herschel

Caroline Herschel's noble auntliness was forged by her partnership with her brother. Born in Hanover, Germany, in 1750,

Caroline was the eighth child of an oboist in the foot guards. Her illiterate mother could not understand why a girl might aspire to anything more than domestic chores, but her father was more encouraging. When he died in 1767, Caroline, age seventeen, was left at the mercy of her mother, who reluctantly allowed her to apprentice herself to a dressmaker. But she dreamed of higher things than that, and eventually followed her adored elder brother William to Bath in England, where he had been appointed organist and director of music in the Octagon Chapel. William primarily wanted Caroline as his housekeeper, but he also had the idea that she could be trained as a professional singer.

It was tough at first. Caroline had little English and felt intimidated by the fashionable folk who milled around the town. Her brother was a hard taskmaster, giving her three singing lessons a day and expecting her to double up with arduous domestic duties, but she soon doggedly succeeded in establishing herself as soprano soloist in the Handel oratorios. But just as her reputation was blossoming, William was losing interest in music and becoming absorbed in astronomy. For this hobby, he needed large telescopes that he built himself, assigning Caroline the exhausting job of polishing the lenses.

Gradually William's hobby became an obsession. All the hours of unclouded darkness were consumed in observations, and Caroline reported that in order to keep her brother "alife [sic], I was even obliged to feed him by putting the vitals by bits into his mouth." By 1781, he had become an expert, discovered the planet Uranus, and been rewarded with a pension from George III. A cottage was granted him near Windsor Castle, and his duties included giving guided tours of the skies to the royal family.

So he abandoned music—and Caroline abandoned her promising singing career, too, to record her brother's celestial observations as well as run his daily life. For twenty years, the rigors were unending. Throughout every night that weather permitted, William would keep his eye to the telescope, calling out what he saw to Caroline, who sat at an adjacent table with a ledger, a clock, and a copy of Flamsteed's atlas of the heavens. It was often dreary labor, but their efforts resulted in the charting of more than twenty-five hundred previously unknown nebulae. And to be fair to William, he insisted that his sister take her share of the honor. In the course of their great research, Caroline became a learned astronomer in her own right, discovering eight comets with the help of a telescope that William had built especially for her. Her revision of Flamsteed's by then quite outdated catalog was published by the Royal Society in 1798, under her own name.

Caroline was granted her own royal pension, and high society began to lionize her. Far from dreary or solitary by temperament, she liked a bit of fun as well as the chance to get out, and she enjoyed these glamorous attentions. But her inner life was discombobulated when William, at the late age of forty-nine, decided to marry a widow. After decades of slavish admiration and loyalty, Caroline felt spurned and wounded and moved into lodgings when William and his new wife went to live in Slough. Fortunately, Mary Herschel proved a thoroughly good thing, and the tensions were happily resolved when she produced a son, John, on whom Caroline instantly doted.

When William died in 1822, Caroline, now seventy-two, made a foolish decision to return to Hanover, where she believed she would soon end her days. But she lived on for another twenty-five years, and according to her first biographer, "'Why did I leave happy England?' was often her cry." Her thoroughly English nephew provided her consolation, the reason to keep living. John Herschel grew into an intellectually prodigious young man who read mathematics at Cambridge and associated himself with Charles Babbage's early experiments in computing, as well as investigating the fields of mechanics, electricity, optics, acoustics, and photography. Caroline fondly recalled witnessing the early signs of his scientific bent.

There were so many paths that this brilliant youth could have taken, but before his death, his father persuaded him to continue in the astronomical line, concentrating on the search for double stars. Caroline herself could no longer observe—her eyes were too old, and where she lived in Hanover "at the heavens there is no getting for the high roofs of the opposite houses"—but she still had the will and the energy to help. With astonishing self-sacrifice, she undertook—at the age of seventy-five—the massive task of reorganizing the catalogs of nebulae. This work was never published, but it won her the Gold Medal of the Astronomical Society.

Ironically, Caroline was forever urging her nephew to cool down and allow himself some of the ordinary life that she had been totally denied in the service of her brother:

> . . . dear nephew, I beg you will consider your health. Encroach not too much on the hours which should be given to sleep. I know how wretched and feverish one feels after two or three nights waking, . . . I should be very sorry on your account, for [sic] if I should not live long enough to know you comfortably married . . . if you can meet with a good-natured, handsome and sensible young lady, pray think of it, and do not wait till you are old and cross.

At least she soon had her way on this last score, and thereafter lived for news of John, his wife, and their children. Of her hundred-pound annual pension, she devoted half to presents for them. In 1832, John took his wife and children to visit her in Hanover. She was eighty-one, he wrote,

> but wonderfully well and very nicely and comfortably lodged; and we have since been on the full trot. She runs

> about the town with me and skips up her two flights of stairs as light and fresh at least as some folks I could name who are not a fourth part of her age . . . in the morning till eleven or twelve she is dull and weary, but as the day advances she gains life, and is quite "fresh and funny" at ten or eleven P.M., and sings old hymns, nay even dances to the great delight of all who see her.

A year later, he took his family off with a large telescope to the clear skies of the Cape of Good Hope. They stayed in South Africa for four years, during which he gathered enormous amounts of fresh astronomical evidence and managed to maintain a lively correspondence with his ever-interested aunt. Eventually came the happy news that he was on his way back to Europe and would take a detour to see her. "So now be sure, dear aunty, and keep yourself well and let us find you in your best looks and spirits."

The reunion was not altogether a success. Aunt fussed over the diet of her delicate great-nephew. "I rather suffered him to hunger than would let him eat anything hurtful," she wrote, "indeed I would not let him eat anything at all without his papa was present." At four o'clock one morning, to avoid tearful farewells, John and his family upped and left without forewarning. Caroline was devastated. The departure, according to her biographer, was "kindly intended, but it was [a] mistake that gave intense pain."

Still, Caroline was not one to lie down and die. Into her nineties, she continued to be active, enjoying the theater, concerts, and opera. Honors unique to women at the time accrued to her: She was awarded honorary membership in the Royal Astronomical Society, and the king of Prussia's Gold Medal for Science was presented to her by the great naturalist Alexander von Humboldt.

Caroline Herschel's career illustrates the limits of possibility for European women in that period. She was someone of no inherited wealth or position who rose to celebrity without access to formal training or advanced educational institutions. Everything she learned was imbibed from William, and her achievement was uncreative, unoriginal, and entirely dependent on his activity. She was essentially a secretary, a drone, a handmaid. "I did nothing for my brother but what a well-trained puppy dog would have done," she admitted, and maybe she felt some bitterness about that.

Anne Jemima Clough

For women of the next generation, more doors were open, and they could begin to act without being entirely beholden to men. Take the case of Anne Jemima Clough, born in 1822, the daughter of a cotton merchant and sister to the brilliant poet Arthur Hugh Clough, one of the golden boys of the early Victorian era who died young, his promise unfulfilled. As a young woman, she taught children and in the 1850s ran a small school in the Lake District where girls were admitted, most unusually, up to the age of sixteen.

A legacy gave her some financial security, and she began to write and think about the problem of extending the education of women beyond the classroom. Among her proposals was a scheme for courses of lectures in higher academic subjects, such as astronomy, to be given by eminent fellows of the universities. These proved such a huge success that she was invited by the reforming Cambridge philosopher Henry Sidgwick to take charge of a house in the town he had acquired to accommodate women attending lectures there. This was the seed of Newnham College, which opened in 1875 and paved the way for the full membership of women in the university.

Despite opposition from die-hard male dons and the scratchiness of Girton College—founded two years earlier on slightly different principles—Newnham expanded rapidly, largely thanks to Anne Clough's fund-raising and irresistible management style. In 1884, her niece Blanche Athena Clough, daughter of the poet, came up to read classics; four years later, Thena (as she was generally known) graduated to become her aunt's secretary. She continued in this post until Anne Clough's death in 1892, after which the younger woman became the college's bursar and wrote a memoir of her aunt, published in 1897.

Here things get a bit complicated. At first glance, the book looks like a typical essay in polite Victorian biography, presenting a carefully edited picture of an endearingly eccentric old lady with magnificent white hair framing huge, heavily lidded dark eyes. "She was above all kind, with an inexhaustible interest in other human beings," writes her niece, radiating "wonderful goodness and sympathy." Wisdom lay in her gaze, she had serenity, tenacity of purpose, and a "power of sustained effort in the face of discouragement." She had no vein of asceticism and no tendency to proselytize: "Enjoy yourself" was one of her most characteristic phrases.

But read Thena's encomium a little closer and you begin to wonder. There is more than a whiff of the satirical backhander in the tone. Anne had "a great deal of the eternal child in her nature," she suffered from "an air of timidity and irresoluteness" . . . she was not learned and her way of talking was rather confused . . . she was wanting in the power of expression and logical arrangement, and she had no gift for expounding general principles . . . she undoubtedly suffered, and was aware that she suffered, from the want of intellectual discipline in youth.

What Thena actually felt was much more violent and negative, as we learn from the enraged, depressive diaries she kept during these years, now part of the Clough–Shore Smith collection in the British Library. "I want to write all I think and know about Aunt Annie," she notes on the opening page of a volume she started just after her aunt's death. "I mean all the piece of her that has been mixed in with me, perhaps I mean all the piece of my experience that has been mixed in with her. . . . I know I don't feel the things everyone expects me to feel."

This was evidently a sensitive matter that festered at the roots of Thena's being. She never set eyes on her father—he was attempting to convalesce in Italy when she was born in England, and he died in Florence only weeks later. His sister Annie then elbowed her way in to help Thena's bereaved young mother cope with both the baby and her infant brother and sister. She continued to regard them proprietarily, personally conducting much of their early schooling and taking them on vacations with her. Thena, it seems, grew up both loving and resenting her domineering yet ineffectual aunt.

Whatever the explanation, the miasma of self-lacerating remorse in Thena's diaries is as ugly as anything in the auntly annals. "The nasty taste of one's own unworthiness is nastier than most things," she moans, and there is indeed something shockingly horrible about a niece expressing so much venom on the figure of a warmly dead old aunt. "I was as her dog," she spits. "Everyone says . . . such a loss to your life. But no one knows I suppose or realizes how I have chafed and champed. . . . Mrs. Sidgwick said she had always supposed it was for my aunt not the college that I stayed—I was taken aback, didn't know the answer. Why it was for myself of course."

She had left home and her sweet-natured but retiring mother to find herself more freedom in what appeared to be the wider world of Newnham, only to find herself "slavecompanionvalet" to a woman whom the world saw through a rosy glow. "To most people she was a friend & sympathizer and helper in their difficulties or a very interesting attractive person whom it was a privilege to see & talk to." But Thena, who dressed and undressed her every day, confronted her "incessant obstinate fussing" and "fidgetting," her quick-tempered snappiness, physical clumsiness, and inability to concentrate—"I know I hadn't cried for years & she used to make me cry with her sharp little words." Without being decisive or efficient, Aunt Annie could not leave well alone: She was a prize interferer, "always so much interested in anything one told her that she made all one's plans for one." Sometimes Thena would have to run off and smoke cigarettes in the fields to filter the stress. On one such stomp, she took a deep breath and told herself that her aunt's "life was more valuable than mine, that to keep her alive was more worth doing than to develop myself, express my own soul."

She tried to live by this epiphany. "I told her I knew I was a troublesome self-willed niece, but I did always really want to do what she wished & she just laughed as she always did when things were getting nearly sentimental." For all the kindness and sympathy she showed to Newnham girls, Aunt Annie was not deeply affectionate. Remarks such as "I make you quite a drudge" or "You'll be quite tired, taking care of your old aunt" or "I like to be where you are, I'm used to you" were the nearest Thena came to gratitude or even recognition that years of her life were being devoured in her aunt's service.

So why did she put up with it? Why did she allow her aunt

to crush her? For an unmarried young woman to be trapped by the iron whims of an elderly relative was of course a common phenomenon of the Victorian era—one thinks of Miss Havisham and Estella in Dickens's *Great Expectations*, of Aunt Stanbury and Dorothy in Trollope's *He Knew He Was Right*, of Aunt Maud and Kate in James's *The Wings of the Dove*. But this drama took place in a milieu in which women were emancipating themselves, and Thena was not without options: She was a highly intelligent and capable young woman who surely had the strength of character, as well as the social and educational status, to tell her aunt that she was going elsewhere.

Did she feel the need to make some sort of propitiatory offering to her dead father, or was her problem the paralyzing lack of self-esteem that colors all her diary confessions? "I have failed badly in all that I aimed at," she writes. "I know really that I am only a carcase bobbing about in the water—tossed hither and thither by circumstance." The antagonism made her examine her conscience with a masochism that was almost Jesuitical in its solipsistic intensity. "I always posed as an oppressed martyr . . . doing jobs without cheerfulness & with a horrid duty doing oppressed air . . . I am always thinking of myself & only think with an effort of other people. This is just the opposite of Annie."

She set herself the hard task of untying this knot by writing her aunt's biography. It's a stiff book, but one that does its subject justice, and after publishing it Thena did at one level move on, finding personal consolation and fulfillment in the creation of the college's beautiful gardens. But she also remained cowering under her aunt's shadow, inasmuch as she stayed at Newnham for more than thirty years after Annie's death—first as treasurer, later as vice principal. In 1911, the blues led her to decline the offer of her aunt's former position as principal, and it was only in 1920 that she finally accepted it, proving to be the outstandingly competent and clearheaded reformer that her aunt had never been.

Both Annie and Thena deserve great honor as founding mothers of university education for women, as well as for their aunt-like nurturing interest in the welfare of generations of Newnham students. The college today contains halls and memorials commemorating the name *Clough*. One wonders how many of the undergraduates who walk past or through them make any mental distinction between aunt and niece—a small ultimate irony that would make Thena smile wryly.

Emma Cons

Another late-Victorian philanthropic spinster aunt who bequeathed her achievement to her niece was the remarkable Emma Cons. And like Annie Clough, Emma Cons was clothed in public-spiritedness rather than institutionalized religion. Born in 1838 into a family prominent in the music trade, she was influenced by the Christian Socialist movement, which was seeking to improve the lot of the poor by uplifting their culture and civilizing their environment.

After attempting to establish an all-female cooperative of watch engravers (on the Swiss model) and working in a stained-glass studio, Emma involved herself in all aspects of housing reform, campaigning for parks, playgrounds, crèches, and clinics as well as sanitary tenements. Her temperament was downright and bluff. Unlike so many other genteel lady do-gooders, she knew how things worked and how they were made and could therefore keep plumbers and tilers on their toes—one suspects that dithering Annie Clough would have infuriated her.

Her great cause, however, was temperance. Appalled by the link between alcohol and domestic violence among the working classes, she established a chain of "coffee taverns" intended to provide conviviality without inebriation and in 1879 raised three thousand pounds to buy a lease on the Victoria Theatre in Waterloo. The area was in a dreadful state, infested with slum housing and brothels, and Miss Cons sought to make what she christened the Royal Victoria Coffee and Music Hall a beacon of moral regeneration, providing not only respectable light entertainment but also a program of lectures and classes. The latter soon gravitated to a site over the road and became the foundation of Morley College, which still flourishes today.

Among the audience at the inaugural performance of the Old Vic, as it came to be affectionately known, was Miss Cons's six-year-old niece Lilian Baylis. A daughter of her sister, Lilian was a musical prodigy, but her aunt was more interested in her administrative skills: From an early age, Lilian was called upon to help with little jobs and fund-raising events at the Vic. Then her family took off to South Africa, where they toured the townships and mining camps as a musical concert party known as the Gipsy Revellers, in which Lilian offered a curious tour de force—skipping while playing the banjo.

In 1897, at the age of twenty-three, her skipping days over, Lilian left her family and returned to London to help her aunt run the Old Vic. Despite royal patronage and the intelligentsia's admiration of an enlightened social experiment, the enterprise had not flourished. "It must not be imagined that the movement to 'elevate the masses' met with immediate success," Lilian later recalled. "On the contrary, the masses showed plainly enough that they did not wish to be elevated." The attractions of low ticket prices and the good clean fun of ballad concerts, operatic excerpts, comic and conjuring turns, Shakespearean recitations, brass bands, and demonstrations of scientific marvels simply could not compensate for the limited appeal of hot beverages and lemonade.

Lilian's starting salary at the Vic was a pound a week, and on this peanut wage she lived with and worked for her aunt for the next fifteen years. Unlike Thena Clough, she felt no resentment at this—in fact, she felt it to be her divine mission, and apart from Sunday morning at church (for she was much more pious than her aunt), she appears to have spent her entire waking life managing the building. This was no easy, sedentary task: She was often called upon to break up brawls, repel the incursions of criminal elements, and brazen it out with the local council when it tried to close the theater for flagrantly breaching health and safety regulations.

Miraculously—and they used to say that she had God on the staff—Lilian Baylis steered the Old Vic through several terminal financial crises and somehow caused it to flourish. Her most far-reaching innovation was a gradual move away from variety toward the establishment of full-scale theatrical and operatic repertory companies. When Miss Cons was on her deathbed in 1912, she knew she was leaving her mission in safe hands. "What about the Vic, Emmie?" Lilian asked.

"You are there, dear," she replied, and then closed her eyes.

Lilian scattered her aunt's ashes in a daffodil wood and hung a picture of her in the Old Vic's foyer, where her likeness was often taken for that of Shakespeare's mother.

After the First World War, the astonishing and magnificent Lilian Baylis continued her aunt's work, although financial exigencies forced her to abandon the principle of temperance. To the Old Vic she added another suburban London theater, Sadler's Wells, and brought dance into the equation. Fat, blunt, myopic, slightly deformed about the mouth, and possessed of a uniquely disagreeable speaking voice, this physically unprepossessing woman, whose aesthetic sensibility was limited, had unknowingly laid the foundations for three great twentieth-century cultural institutions now known as the National Theatre, the English National Opera, and the Royal Ballet.

Later in her life—she died in 1937, having become a legend in her lifetime—her nephew Robert returned from South Africa. Even though she more resembled some stalwart old carthorse, he called her Auntie Tiger. Sadly, according to her biographer, "She was too bossy and formidable to win his affection." Good nieces do not always make good aunts.

The Lion Aunt

Lack of a husband didn't stop most aunts from cheerfully getting on with it. In the years before the First World War, the British poet Stevie Smith was largely brought up by an aunt who came to run the household when Stevie's father ran away to sea. Stevie's mother was overwhelmed and Stevie herself sickly, but Aunt Maggie was, in Stevie's words, "strong, happy, simple, shrewd, staunch, loving, upright and bossy," and sorted both of them out.

There is no story to her life. Her pleasures were the perusal of the law reports in *The Times* and a visit to the local church, where she was wardrobe mistress for the boys' choir. Otherwise her days were filled with the domestic round and the quiet, firm, reciprocated love of her clever oddball niece, in whose writings she took auntly pride rather than intellectual interest. Stevie compares her to "shining gold" and "a lion with a spanking tail who will have no nonsense." As Stevie's biographer Frances Spalding puts it, "Compared with her love for her aunt, all other intimate relationships in Stevie's life were abortive."

As the Lion Aunt declined into dotage, the roles were reversed, and Stevie uncomplainingly fetched and cooked and carried for a bedridden old lady. Aunt Maggie died after a stroke in 1968, at the age of ninety-six. In effect, this left her niece widowed. "I know [it's] best really, because she would never have been happy or comfortable again," Stevie writes, "but all the same, it is awful. . . . I think in her mind I always remained the rather feeble child I was when she first came to take charge of us all. But I always told her—and how truthfully!—that I depended on her just as much as she did on me."

THE FAMILY POPE

Carolyn Heinze, thirty, is a freelance writer and editor based in Paris. She grew up in Welland, Ontario, a small blue-collar town near Niagara Falls and the US border. She remembers her spinster aunt Bea:

My uncle Malcolm says that the problem with Aunt Bea is that she is in dire need of a good, well . . . you-know-what. Christened (behind her back, of course) the Family Pope, Aunt Bea, who is well into her seventies, has never married, never had children, and has lived as, what those from another time would label it, a spinster.

Before she retired, Auntie Bea worked at the city hall in the small town where I grew up—a town of factories and tradesmen and a polluted canal running through it. If it weren't for the canal (and the construction of a gargantuan Wal-Mart that has, as the store has done in so many other sleepy locales, ripped the community of a once quaint and thriving center), there really wouldn't be any reason for the town to exist.

But Aunt Bea saw things differently. In her post at city hall, she toiled away to promote her home, conscientiously fulfilling her duties at the office and, in her spare time, launching initiatives to bring attention to what she believed to be a perfectly good destination—not the cemetery of dead inspiration her more angst-ridden teenage nieces and nephews deemed it to be. One memorable project involved the commissioning of local artists to paint murals depicting moments drawn from the town's history. These oeuvres, my aunt argued, would boost the community's nonexistent tourism industry.

The more urban-minded in her circle merely laughed at Auntie Bea: Who in their right mind would go out of their way to see a bunch of oversize gas station art in the armpit of a region that had so much more to offer? Sadly, their skepticism proved sound: Few tourists meander through the city's quiet streets, and the murals, faded and crumbling, remain a reminder of this well-intentioned failure.

In fact, people were always laughing at Aunt Bea. It's true, her rigidity and compartmentalized organization were always a bit amusing, and at times extremely frustrating. The type of person who grew anxious if there was one unanswered piece of correspondence on her desk, she probably drove her co-workers nuts. She certainly drove our family crazy. In her role as the archetypical spinster, Auntie Bea couldn't relate to those whose responsibilities extended past work and housekeeping to husbands, wives, children, family meals, piano lessons, and after-school sports—and all of the harried rushing around that accompanies these.

But spinsters have their responsibilities, too, and Aunt Bea fulfilled these with a career soldier's sense of duty. When my great-grandmother proved too senile to live alone, it was Aunt Bea who housed her, tending to the mundane and sometimes messy tasks related to caring for the elderly. When my own mother was on her deathbed, too weak to continue her battle against cancer, it was Aunt Bea who filled in at the hospital when my father—exhausted and weary and pulled in a million different directions—went to check on my sister and me.

At Christmastime, Aunt Bea always threw a party, doling out lavish presents to all the kids. The gifts, obviously chosen with care and taste, weren't the electronic gadgets that we were accustomed to receiving from our younger relatives, but, for me at least, they produced their own little thrills. My very first magazine subscription—so grown up!—arrived courtesy of Auntie Bea, and I will never look at an issue of Reader's Digest *without thinking of her.*

Family members often joke that if no one is either sick or dying, Aunt Bea isn't happy. Everyone knows that she has struggled with bouts of depression all of her life. And it always seems to hit her when, on a practical level, she isn't needed. I always thought it unfair to think that Aunt Bea drew her energy from the misery and suffering of others.

As far as the family knows, Auntie Bea has never been in love. There was a gentleman caller once—I remember them coming over to our house for cocktails. He was nice, charming, good looking for an old guy, I remember thinking at the time. But things didn't last between them. "Maybe he tried to get too serious," my cousin joked, her remark dripping with sexual innuendo.

Maybe. I hope so. Hopefully, this forgotten suitor was so head-over-heels that he couldn't stand it. Because more than Auntie Bea is in need of a good you-know-what, she yearns to be needed. And, for once in her life, perhaps she was needed not because of her nurturing skills, but just because she was Aunt Bea.

KALA SHAMOO

Sarmad Sehbai, a young man who lives in Pakistan, on his aunt Shamoo:

I belong to Kashmir, the land disputed between Pakistan and India. Kashmir is also very near to Sialkot, which is now in Pakistan. We have large families. I have six aunts, born and raised at a time when women were not encouraged to educate themselves. Simple reading and writing was thought to be enough for them, and they would be married off at fifteen or sixteen; my mother was married at fourteen.

Shamoo was the youngest sister of all. We lovingly call her Kala, which means "auntie," and Shamoo, which is short for Shamima, meaning "fragrance." Between my mother and her, there was not much age difference, so they were quite close to each other. Being the youngest, they had had a naughty bone.

We don't socialize much outside of the clan, because our family is so big. Every day there are festivities going on, eating at someone's place—your place, my place. Everyone has the same style of generosity—treating twelve people or twenty people unannounced. You can just go to their house and be entertained.

My earliest memories of Kala Shamoo are of her at weddings. She's a lovely singer, she sings folk wedding songs and dances in a beautiful manner, though dancing isn't very much approved of in our family.

Kala Shamoo is very lively. She loves dancing, laughing, and cooking, but she is very politically aware, too. Her husband was pro-Russia, a communist. Although my auntie is not educated or an intellectual, she has an acute sense of national politics. She believed in the People's Party of Pakistan, founded by Zulfikar Ali Bhutto. Both my mother and she went on this movement for restoration of democracy in Lahore, protesting against General Zia-ul-Haq, the military ruler in the 1980s who had hanged Bhutto.

As the procession was tear-gassed, this intelligence man from the police in plainclothes, bald and respectable, came up to my mother and aunt. "You are very nice ladies," he said. "There is tear gas and a baton charge—why don't you step aside, sit in my car, and I can take you to a safe place?" So the two sisters, mistaking him for a sympathizer, went and sat in the car. But this man took them to the jail: This seeming gentleman was in fact a cop. My aunt and mother gave him hell: "You nude-headed bastard, a minute ago you were calling us sisters and now we have become criminals? You are a cheat! You are an agent of General Zia-ul-Haq!" The poor man didn't know how to react to their fury.

In prison, my mother and aunt started dancing and painting walls with anti–General Zia slogans and cartoons. They made the lives of the guards miserable by turning the whole affair into a picnic. No surprise, they both were sentenced to prison for a month or so.

My relationship with my aunt is very loving. Since I lost my mother, she reminds me of her, especially as they were so close to each other. Kala Shamoo's husband was an engineer. They used to move from one place to another and when they finally settled in Lahore, there was a daily ritual of mother and Kala visiting each other's homes. When Kala's husband died recently, I went to see her and she was sitting in the women's quarter—men and women don't normally sit side by side. I kissed her on the cheek. She was very calm and composed. Now I'm based in Islamabad and she's in Lahore, and whenever I'm in Lahore we usually meet at weddings, parties, funerals. There are no expectations, no compulsory meetings, but it's a normal ritual thing that whenever I'm in Lahore; somehow or other we will meet.

Except for my mother and my aunt, nobody else in my family ever got involved in politics. The other aunts are married to rather richer husbands and are ladies of leisure. My aunt has probably seen more of life than the others. The best thing about her is that she is not intimidated or impressed by any pretension, pomp, show, or posturing. She comes forth very simple but not without substance, and never afraid of anything.

Our relationship does not change. If I met her at a wedding now, I'd just hug her and ask her "Could we have this dance?" She would probably say, "My knees are not supporting me, I'm too fat for it." And I would insist, and suddenly she would start dancing. I wish I could visit her more often, hug her more often, make her stand on her two feet and dance like that.

MARIA ALTMANN: PORTRAIT OF A HEROIC NIECE

Maria Altmann, now in her nineties and living in Los Angeles, belongs in the annals of great niecedom for her fight to honor and reclaim for her family the paintings depicting her late aunt Adele Bloch-Bauer, as well as other Klimt masterpieces.

Altmann, who was born in 1916, fled Nazi Austria and eventually settled in Hollywood, California. She is the niece of Czech sugar tycoon Ferdinand Bloch, who owned artwork by the renowned Austrian painter Gustav Klimt, including two portraits of Bloch's wife, Adele Bloch-Bauer. These paintings

Portrait of Adele Bloch-Bauer I
Oil on canvas, by Gustav Klimt, 1907

were seized by the Nazis; five of them wound up in the hands of the Austrian government. In 2000, Altmann sued to get the paintings back and eventually won. In June 2006, Altmann sold the painting *Portrait of Adele Bloch-Bauer I* (shown) to cosmetics magnate and art collector Ronald S. Lauder for $135 million, the highest price ever paid for a painting. In November 2006, the painting *Adele Bloch-Bauer II* (1912) sold at auction in New York City for eighty-eight million dollars.

4

X-RATED AUNTS

In my student days, I remember a Casanova-type friend confiding that he prevented his physical ardor from reaching an overhasty conclusion by forcing himself to envision a row of full trash cans. A lineup of his elderly aunts might well have performed a similar function, for sex and aunts just don't go together. Indeed, they seem to cancel each other out.

Yet of all the stereotypes that characterize the breed, there is perhaps none so vivid as the pathetically shriveled maiden aunt who conceives a hopeless crush on a man younger and more attractive than she is. There are many examples in literature and film in which the maiden aunt faces grotesque humiliation when she dares to give way to romantic feelings and physical yearnings.

But there is another role an aunt can play, one that presents her in a more alluring light—as the initiator into the world of adult pleasures. In Colette's short story "Gigi" (1944), the teenage heroine is groomed by her aunt Alicia, an elderly courtesan whose attitudes are entirely worldly. Alicia is scheming for Gigi to be set up as the mistress of Gaston, the playboy son of her former amour, and in anticipation of her forthcoming pampered existence spends hours teaching the girl the finer points of table manners, such as the proper way to eat lobster. But all Aunt Alicia's best-laid plans go ironically wrong when Gaston and Gigi reject the morality of their forefathers by falling in love and deciding to get married.

For aunts and nephews, initiation can take a more physical turn, with the nephew's adolescent libido taking the lead. Their sexual intercourse is not always against the law. Incest between aunt and nephew is not a strongly defined taboo, though the source of all Judeo-Christian legislation, Leviticus 18, where the Lord spake unto Moses, decrees (in verses 12 and 13):

> Thou shalt not uncover the nakedness of thy father's sister; she is thy father's near kinswoman.
>
> Thou shalt not uncover the nakedness of thy mother's sister; for she is thy near kinswoman.

Almost universally, a niece or nephew is forbidden from marrying an aunt or uncle to whom they have any blood relation or "consanguinity"—the principal exception being the strongly matrilineal Trobriand Islands, where sexual relations with a father's sister are not considered incestuous. Equally widespread is the freedom to marry a widowed or divorced aunt or uncle to whom there is no blood link. Hence Mario Vargas Llosa's novel *Aunt Julia and the Scriptwriter* (1998) isn't as scandalous as it sounds. It's really only the Stendhalian-Colettesque tale of a guileless young man in love with a sophisticated older woman—the hero, a minor, ends up marrying his uncle's wife's sister, an aunt only by extension of the normal usage.

Shakespeare's Hamlet, already suffering from a bad case of the Oedipus complex, is further confused when his widowed mother, Gertrude, marries his late father's brother Claudius, making them "my uncle-father and aunt-mother," as he puts it to Rosencrantz and Guildenstern (*Hamlet,* II.ii).

Pornographic literature doesn't get as excited about incest along the aunt–nephew axis as it does about mother–son or brother–sister relations, but it's a lively enough fantasy nonetheless, as the thousands of true-life confessions on many repellent modern Web sites illustrate. Somewhat more engaging in tone is *Forbidden Fruit,* a novel dating from 1898, in which pretty young Aunt Gertie arrives to look after her twelve-year-old nephew Percy, a lad with one thing on his mind. Owing to the smallness of the house, he is obliged to share his bedroom with her. After the light has been turned out, she creeps in. "What a beautiful boy," she coos over his bed, thinking him to be asleep. "If only I dared . . ." and kisses him, waking him up.

So one thing leads to another, and eventually aunt and nephew are locked in intimate congress. "Percy, push yourself closer to me, it's so nice, my darling," whispers Aunt Gertie.

"A kind of rage possessed me," Percy recalls. "I wanted to kill her by thrusting my instrument as savagely as possible."

Following a climax and detumescence, Percy moans, "Oh Auntie, you've killed me, it's gone dead now."

"Don't call me Auntie" she replies. "Call me Gertie. Say you love me, Percy, but never tell anyone what we have done tonight."

After further copulation and some playful spanking, Gertie

cries, "Percy what a champion you are," and christens him "Mr. Pego." But the triumphant Percy now has another conquest in mind—his even more lubricious mother. Enough said.

From 1909 to 1911, desperately attempting to make some money at the beginning of his literary career, Guillaume Apollinaire wrote several essays in pornography, now considered by connoisseurs to be little gems of erotica. "So limpidly perverse, so fragrant with young private perfumes that one wonders if it may not be another of [his] anti-Symbolist sallies," writes his biographer Francis Steegmuller of *Les exploits d'un jeune Don Juan*. Roger, a wealthy pubescent, is sent to live in a deserted château with his mother, sisters, and aunt. In childhood, he had been bathed one evening by his twenty-six-year-old aunt Marguerite, ten years younger than his mother. "I remember vividly that every time my Aunt Marguerite washed and dried my genitals I was conscious of an unfamiliar vague but extremely pleasant sensation," he writes.

> And I kissed her pretty cherry-red lips behind which sparkled her beautiful white teeth.
>
> As soon as I was out of the bath, I begged her to dry me. So my aunt dried me, lingering perhaps even longer than was necessary over my sensitive areas.

At that point, prim Aunt Marguerite decides that the fun has gone far enough. But Roger wants more—"Be a nice auntie and have a bath with me some time." Auntie resists, at which Roger resorts to blackmail: "If you don't, I'll tell Daddy that you've put my thing in your mouth again."

> My aunt blushed deeply. As a matter of fact, she really had done that, but only for a second, one day when I had not wanted to take my bath. The water had been too cold and I'd run off to my room to hide. My aunt had come looking for me and at length had taken my tiny penis into her mouth, squeezing it between her lips for a second. I had enjoyed it so much that I had finally relented and become as docile as a lamb.

Eventually, to keep the boy quiet, Aunt Marguerite agrees to get into the bath alone. Roger helps her to dry and dress. As he reaches her knees, however, she stops him, and henceforth he and his aunt take their baths separately. But a few days later, Roger overhears her in the confessional, admitting in low and hesitant tones:

> that although she had never before felt any carnal desires, she had been moved to emotion upon seeing her young

> nephew in his bath, and had lustfully touched his body, but fortunately had been able to master these wicked desires. Except once when her nephew was sleeping; the blanket had slipped off the bed, leaving his genitals exposed. She had stood there looking at him for a long time and had even taken his member into her mouth.

Some weeks later, after he has had his way with several other ladies of low estate, Roger discovers his aunt in the château's library, reading the entry in the encyclopedia for "onanism" and looking at the *Atlas of Anatomy*.

> I pretended not to notice her embarrassment, and said to her softly: "You too must get bored sometimes, auntie dear. The priest who lived here before had quite a collection of interesting books dealing with the problems of human life. Why don't you take some with you to your room?"
>
> I took two and slipped them into her pocket: *Marriage Unveiled* and *Love and Marriage*. When she affected reluctance, I added: "Naturally, this is between you and me and the gatepost: We're not children are we, auntie?" And I suddenly seized her and gave her a resounding kiss.

The boy is soon transported with ardor, and Marguerite is forced to resist his advances again. But when they next meet alone, the citadel falls. Roger slips into her bedroom and he blurts out his passion for her. "Let us be husband and wife, beautiful, darling Marguerite." She succumbs, and what follows is "a brief encounter, but one whose sensations were infinite," which "brought both of us to the limit of the most frenzied ecstasy." After this first bout, they are immediately at it again, in "a long battle during which we perspired through every pore in our bodies. Shouting like a mad woman, she was the first to reach the climax. Mine felt so good that it almost hurt. That was enough; we separated."

At the novel's conclusion, it is revealed that both the aunt and another of Roger's conquests are pregnant. Husbands are found to make their position respectable, and Roger continues to enjoy extramarital sessions with both of them. Apollinaire, in case you are wondering, didn't have an aunt.

Such is the stuff of idle masturbatory fantasy. To find a truly perceptive account of the relationship between an aunt and a nephew, we must turn to Stendhal's rambling but enthralling novel *La chartreuse de Parme* (*The Charterhouse of Parma*), published in 1839. It's the story of a young nobleman called Fabrice del Dongo, who returns to his home in northern Italy after fighting for Napoleon at Waterloo. He comes back covered with some sort of glory, and his mother's sister Gina—the Countess Pietranera, and then on her remarriage the duchess of Sanseverina, a woman of beauty, vivacity, intelligence, and will—is enchanted by him. No, more than enchanted—disarmed and confused. Not having any children of her own, she had adored Fabrice as a boy, but now she adores him as a handsome young man, and something uncontrollable enters her emotion, something she cannot openly acknowledge.

A more striking transgression of the taboo is provided by Charlotte Mendelson's *Love in Idleness* (2001), a rather vapid novel written from a lesbian perspective in a manner that lies uneasily between Margaret Drabble and Bridget Jones. Anna is a goofy graduate who doesn't really know much about herself. She finds her middle-class family very irritating and can't wait to get away from home. Only her mother's feline sister Stella holds any sort of fascination for her—the fascination of glamour. Stella's lips look "as soft as marzipan," and her "long, cool, crescent-lidded eyes . . . pin you smiling in their gaze." In personality, she is "famous for her sneer . . . ironic, unimpressed, and somewhat dangerous, she is never nice for effect, unlike her sister, who doesn't have the courage to be seriously rude." Mostly she lives in Paris, where she is involved in filmmaking, and she offers Anna the use of her Bloomsbury house while she is away.

Anna accepts with delight and arrives in London, where she finds a job in a bookshop. But she finds the house-sitting unnerving, not least because of the baffling clues she picks up about her aunt's love life, including a photograph of her amorously entwined with another woman. Eventually, Anna meets up with someone she assumes to be Stella's boyfriend, but he makes it clear that this is not the case: Stella is a mystery wrapped inside an enigma.

Stella finally returns to the London house, and she and Anna spend the evening together, talking and drinking as the atmosphere gets headier. What follows might just be the world's first-ever aunt–niece clinch—groundbreaking, if not earth-shattering:

> There is a hand on her waist, and her own palm rests on a fluttering curve of skin. She stands on an island, in a storm of fireballs, shooting stars and lightning—a soft electric collision of lips and figures. . . .
>
> Anna is appalled at herself.
>
> Her mother's sister.
>
> Her mother's *sister*.
>
> Not just her relative.
>
> But female.

AUNT VICKI

Auntliness is most often associated with comfort—even an agony aunt (see page 204) assuages the pain. Aunt Vicki, an interesting exception to the rule, lives near the Fort Worth airport in Texas. Her Web site informs us that she is "an experienced, strict but understanding, stern but loving disciplinarian." A photograph of a plain, plump middle-aged woman in glasses with a slightly exasperated expression does indeed seem to embody these qualities—she could be a librarian or a primary-school teacher. But the sort of comfort this aunt offers is exquisitely and deliberately painful: In her hand she clutches a wooden implement the size of a Ping-Pong paddle, and the caption reads, "You—get over here—NOW!"

For Aunt Vicki "loves to spank," and she is "very good at it," too. "I use the over-the-knee position as well as a spanking stool. . . . There's nothing more satisfying than the feel of my hairbrush or paddle smacking a naughty bare bottom," she continues. Together with Aunt Prissy—her sister, it is claimed, though the photograph suggests a male transvestite—she runs a service designed to satisfy a common sexual fantasy whose most celebrated modern exegete was perhaps the critic Kenneth Tynan.

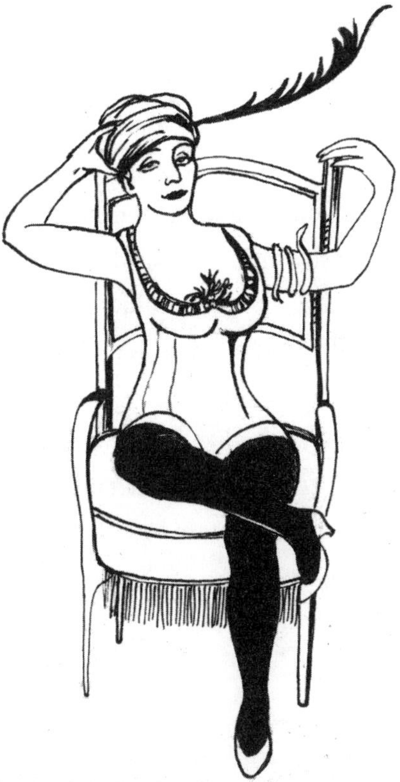

"I have been a strict disciplinarian most of my life, beginning with helping to raise my brothers and sisters, and then raising my own children," she says. "And now I have continued to administer discipline when needed, in the form of corporal punishment, combined with scolding, corner time, humiliation, panty training and more." Using hairbrushes, straps, belts, canes, crops, rulers, and wooden spoons, she administers "spanking, paddling, caning, whipping, strapping, switching and any other method that seems effective. . . . When you have a spanking session with me you will certainly feel you have been punished."

Aunt Vicki is not, she insists, "a leather dominatrix"; what she provides is "domestic-style discipline . . . I am not sadistic, but I am firm and will spank as hard as the situation calls for." The premises of her "spanking house" contain a schoolroom and a sheriff's office, and she has "plans to build an authentic woodshed out the back so that I really can take some of you 'out to the woodshed.' If anyone wants to help with labor and/or materials, then contact me."

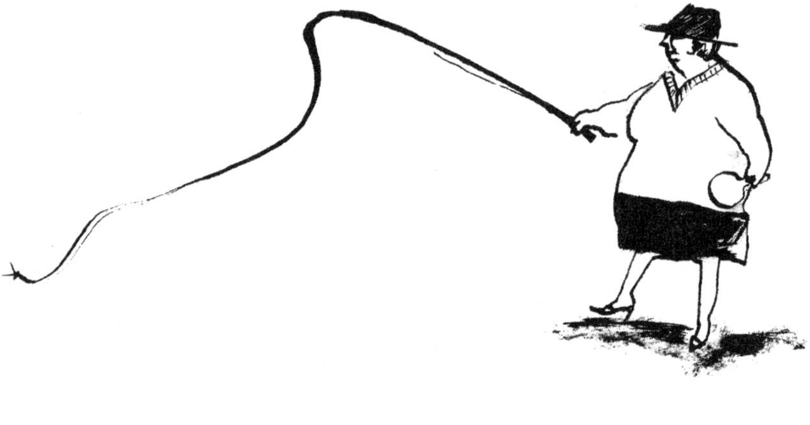

Aunt Vicki's gifts find her besieged. Those who crave a domestic-style whacking must fill in a questionnaire and send her a fifty-dollar deposit, but she warns that it may be months before she can deal with you. Meanwhile, people write in and chat. A thirty-two-year-old woman from Florida, for example, says: "I have a very young sweet face and a soft white backside. Generally, I'm very loving and generous, but sometimes I get too self-centered. Last naughty thing I did . . . I forgot to pay all my bills on time. How would you handle a girl like me?" Aunt Vicki responds by offering the prospect of a good purgative thrashing with a hairbrush.

ROCK-'N'-ROLL AUNTS

Gigolo Aunts is an indie rock band formed in 1986 in Boston, Massachusetts. Previously called Sniper, Marauder, and Rosetta Stone, they took the name Gigolo Aunts from an incomprehensible psychedelic song by the mysterious Syd Barrett, one of the founding fathers of Pink Floyd.

The band was little known until 1992. An album of original songs called *Where I Find My Heaven* was its biggest success. The title track was used in both the gross-out movie *Dumb and Dumber* and as the theme tune to a BBC sitcom called *Game On*.

The band has suffered many ups and downs, but its artistic emphasis has constantly remained on emotional and musical clarity, pitched very loud. The Gigolo Aunts' most recent album was *Minor Chords and Major Themes,* released in 2003. Since then, the group appears to have disbanded.

SCISSOR SISTERS

In a recent interview, Jake Shears, the lead singer of the American band Scissor Sisters, paid homage to a recently deceased aunt. He says "that he was deeply affected by the recent death of a beloved aunt. He had used her last words to him—"When you cut the lights out, think of me" in a song called "Lights." "I felt sombre," he says, "but it turned into a slutty disco number." A touching sentiment, especially from a group named for a sexual position between two women.

5

BRAND-NAME AUNTS

For Americans, the idea of an aunt as "any benevolent practical woman who exercises these qualities to the benefit of her circle of acquaintances" has been persistent. This might explain the widespread commercial exploitation of the word, and especially its association with home-spun, home-grown, home-cooked goods you can trust.

An auntly product will treat, not cheat you: Solidly and traditionally made, it is more concerned with old-fashioned substance than newfangled style. Tried and tested in the kitchen rather than the factory, it is suitable for universal family consumption. Like *community* and *organic,* the word *aunt* has no adverse connotation.

AUNT JEMIMA

The most celebrated auntly product in the United States—on a par with Betty Crocker and Ronald McDonald—may be Aunt Jemima Pancake Mix (nowadays Pancake & Waffle Mix and owned by the Pepsi Corporation). This stuff has an interesting history. It was launched by the Pearl Milling Company in 1889 and named after a popular vaudeville song of the day. The picture on the box depicted a Southern mammy—drawn, in fact, from an African American woman from Chicago called Nancy Green—who became the very stereotype of the loyal and cheerful black servant, wearing a broad smile and a bandanna around her head. "Honey, it's easy to be de sweetheart o you' family," read early advertising copy. "Yo' know how de men folks an' de young folks all loves my tasty pancakes. An yo' can make dem fo' dem jiffy-quick, an' jus' right every time, wid my magic ready-mix."

Nancy Green demonstrated this early convenience food (dried milk was the secret ingredient) in person at the Chicago World's Fair of 1893, causing such a sensation that the police had to be called in to control the crowds. Dressed as Aunt Jemima, she continued to tour the country for the next thirty years promoting the mix, which was bought out in 1926 by Quaker Oats.

With the advent of the civil rights movement in the 1960s, the image of Aunt Jemima began to be perceived as insultingly servile, and she was redrawn slimmer and younger. In 1989, she was given a complete makeover and made into an "aspirational" buppie (black upwardly mobile professional), losing the stigma of the bandanna and given a fashionable coiffure, pearl earrings, and a lacy collar instead.

Aunt Jemima, Then and Now: From the Offensive to the Politically Correct

The Aunt Jemima trademark started in 1893, and the pancake mix debuted in 1889. In 1926, Quaker Oats bought the brand, and the frozen products were licensed to Pinnacle Foods in 1996. Her image has changed over the years, from a plump, smiling woman with a kerchief over her hair, like a mammy or slave, to a younger, slimmer, attractive woman with well-coiffed hair and tasteful pearls. An early, non-politically-correct ad contained the following copy: "On the old plantation, Aunt Jemima refused to reveal to a soul the secret of those light fragrant pancakes which she baked for her master and his guests. Only once, long after her master's death did Aunt Jemima

Aunt Jemima portrayer Anna Robinson, photographed between 1933 and 1951

reveal her recipe. . . ." In the popular vernacular, the phrase *Aunt Jemima* refers to a servile black woman, the female equivalent of an Uncle Tom.

AN ARRAY OF AUNTLY STUFF

A trawl of Google reveals many other American auntly products, dividing largely into three categories:

Crafts and Antiques

Aunt Billie's Unique Handmade Gifts
Aunt Flossie's Attic
Aunt Annie's Crafts
Aunt Helen's Handicrafts
Aunt Mary's Yarns
Auntie Em's Dollhouses and Accessories
Aunt Lois' Homemade Soap
Aunt Judy's Attic
Aunt Sue's Country Corner
Aunt Annie's Quilt Nook
Auntie's Homespun Crafts

Prepared Foods and Recipes

Aunt Libby's Kitchen
Aunt Leah's Fudge
Aunt Betty's Steamed Puddings
Aunt Minnie's Southern Style Entrees and Desserts
Aunt Sally's Original Creole Pralines
Auntie Joe's Gourmet Gift Baskets
Aunt Selma's Chocolates
Aunt Ellie's Borscht
Aunt Ruby's Peanuts
Aunt Nellie's Pickled Beets
Aunt Wanda's Turkey Carcass Soup
Aunt Lizzie's Gourmet Cheese Straws
Aunt Gussie's Country Delectables
Aunt Viola's Best Doggone Caesar Dressing
Aunt Jem's Home Made Frozen Raw Pet Food
Auntie Anne's Pretzels

Bed-and-Breakfasts

Aunt Sadie's, the Ozarks, Missouri
Aunt Olly's, Rhode Island
Aunt Suzie's, Pennsylvania

Aunt Martha's, Florida
Auntie's House, Amarillo, Texas
Aunt Daisie's, Illinois
Aunt Rebecca's, Baltimore, Maryland
Aunt Peg's, St. Augustine, Florida
Aunt Irma's, Ohio

AUNT BEE OF MAYBERRY

The Andy Griffith Show ran for eight seasons, starting in 1960, with 249 episodes produced. It was number one in the Nielsen ratings in its final year, and during its run was never out of the top ten most watched—and beloved shows—in America. Even today, it continues to be a favorite on cable reruns.

The show is set in Mayberry, a fictional small town in North Carolina. The main character is Sheriff Andy Taylor (Griffith), who lives with his Aunt Bee (Frances Bavier) and adorable young son Opie (Ron Howard). Andy's loyal deputy is the high-strung Barney Fife (Don Knotts).

Aunt Bee resembles everyone's favorite aunt—nurturing, kind, a great housekeeper and cook, with a mind of her own. Her cooking was celebrated, as this excerpt from *The Andy Griffith Show Book* by Ken Beck and Jim Clark (St. Martin's Press) explains:

> Andy once told his aunt that she should be called Miss Fried Chicken of Mayberry. Every Sunday, she prepares either fried chicken or roast beef for dinner. Among her specialties are rhubarb pie and homemade strawberry ice cream (from an old family recipe), both of which have won blue ribbons at the county fair. . . . Another of Aunt Bee's special dishes is ham loaf with green beans Chinese style.

Andy Griffith and Frances Bavier, in *The Andy Griffith Show* (1960–1968)

She got the recipe from the *Mayberry Gazette*, but because she lined the garbage pail with the newspaper, she had to guess about the final ingredients. . . . Once, her cold leftovers served as a midnight feast for visiting American and Russian dignitaries who were in Mayberry for a summit meeting. It was her handsome victuals that paved the way for peace. As the diplomats prepared to leave, it was only natural for Bee to give them some leftover fried chicken in a brown paper sack for the road.

Aunt Bee's Mayberry Cookbook by Ken Beck and Jim Clark (Rutledge Hill Press), first published in 1991, has sold close to a million copies to date and is chock-full of down-home Southern recipes.

AUNT BEE'S FRIED CHICKEN

1 frying chicken
2 eggs, beaten
All-purpose flour
Shortening

Wash and cut up the chicken. Dip the pieces in the beaten egg, season with salt, and roll in the flour. Put a right smart amount of shortening in a frying pan and melt it. When it's good and hot, turn it down a little and fry the chicken slowly. Turn the chicken pieces over 3 to 4 times and cook slowly for about 15 or 20 minutes. After it gets brown, put a lid over the chicken and simmer for 20 minutes.

Serves 4 to 6.

AUNT BEE'S SPOON BREAD

1¾ cups boiling water
¾ cup sifted cornmeal
2 tablespoons butter
2 eggs, 3 if small
1¼ cups milk
1 teaspoon salt
1 teaspoon baking powder

In the top of a double boiler over simmering water, pour the boiling water over the cornmeal. Stir constantly until thick and smooth, about 5 minutes. Add the butter and blend until melted. Let the mixture cool.

Grease a medium-sized baking dish. Beat the eggs and add the milk and salt. Stir the egg mixture into the cornmeal mixture. Beat until well mixed. Add the baking powder and beat well. Turn into the prepared dish. Bake in a 425 degree oven for 45 minutes, until firm but still moist.

Serves 4 to 5.

CONTINENTAL AUNTS

Cynical Europeans don't buy into the auntly guarantee of quality with the same fervor as Americans. In Germany, a Tante Paula is a form of motorized scooter—but apart from a scattering of restaurants called Tante this or that, the idea of the aunt is not a big selling point. Except perhaps in Belfast, where Aunt Mollie's Quality Foods produces crumble mixture and ready-rolled pastry (puff and shortcrust), and Aunt Sandra's Candy Factory is a little patch of sweet heaven, with lollipops, fudge, and toffee apples. Almost all these aunts are, of course, mere figments of an ad man's imagination, but Aunt Sandra has a corporeal existence: She established the factory in 1953 and has now handed it over to her nephew David Moore.

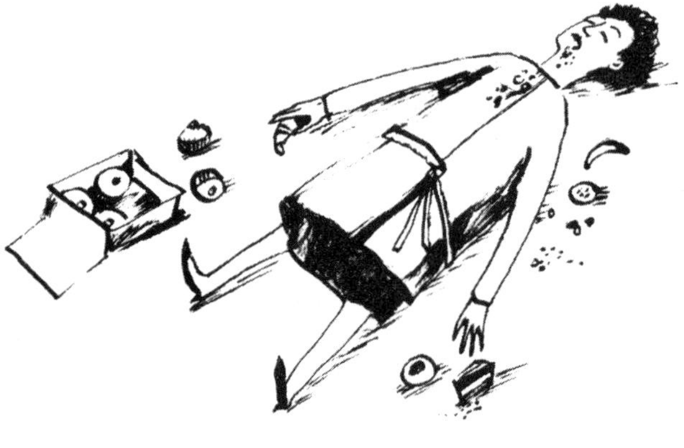

AUNTS FOR HIRE

In Britain, the most celebrated branding of the aunt comes in the shape of a pioneering employment agency, which made its reputation on the strength of its impeccable gentility and respectability. This was the brainchild of Gertrude Maclean, a scion of a large Edwardian clan whose seven brothers and sisters were scattered in commanding positions over the globe. Gertrude was the one who stayed at home, unable to bag a husband in the terrible dearth of young men that followed the carnage of the First World War. Meanwhile, her siblings bundled their offspring back to England to be educated, and Gertrude's role was to pick them up from ports and railway stations, deliver them to schools, and look after them during vacations. She was an ace aunt, by all accounts, "a rock and a sport," playful and affectionate, and as her nieces and nephews all began to outgrow her, she decided in 1921 to continue her activities on a commercial basis and establish a business she called Universal Aunts.

Her timing was perfect. War had put an end to the bottomless pool of residential domestic servants. Women may have had less chance of marrying, but they now had the vote, their first Member of Parliament, more chance of entering the professions—and shorter skirts and fewer corsets. It became not only respectable, but also economically necessary for the middle class of unmarried or widowed women to seek remunerative work, so long as it wasn't demeaning physically. To be a Universal Aunt was to be at once useful and independent without losing caste.

The advertisement in *The Times* read:

UNIVERSAL AUNTS
(LADIES OF IRREPROACHABLE BACKGROUND)
CARE OF CHILDREN
CHAPERONAGE
HOUSE FURNISHING
SHOPPING FOR THE COLONIES
RESEARCH WORK

Working out of a tiny room off Sloane Street in the mornings and conducting interviews on sofas in Harrods Ladies' Rest Room in the afternoons, Gertrude Maclean (under the nom de guerre of Miss Safrana Fort) offered to do "anything for anyone at any time"—short of prostitution or marriage brokering. Most of her clients required escorts ("proxy parents") for their children, but advice on interior decoration and How to Get On in Society were also much in demand. There was no shortage of labor, with notes kept on all applicants. For example:

MISS ELIZABETH PRATT-STEED
Disciplinarian. Firm without being brutal. Can converse on physics, spiritualism or foreign missions. Not a time-waster, good cheap aunt.

MRS. CHARLOTTE HEDGECOMBE
Age 55

Hefty, stern, stands no nonsense. Stickler for etiquette and deportment. On Borstal Board of Governors, Zoological Society's certificate. Cope older boys, any number.

Universal Aunts went on to become an imperial institution, claiming on its eightieth anniversary to have employed "over three quarters of a million men and women and undertaken over a million services." Even in Blair-ite Britain, it continued to flourish, taking a pride in discreetly meeting the outlandish requests of oil sheikhs and Russian billionaires without turning a pink-rinsed hair. Nice country-reared girls, with a practical rather than intellectual bent and the stamp of finishing school upon their brains, form the backbone of its staff: In the late 1970s, one Lady Diana Spencer spent time on its books, working with children.

6

EXOTIC AND ECCENTRIC AUNTS

Imperious and impetuous, yet brusquely kind and briskly sensible with her "quick, bright eye," mobcap, and gentleman's watch, Betsy Trotwood provides a template for the benignly eccentric Victorian aunt. A contented spinster leading a life of militant independence, she takes in her orphaned nephew David Copperfield when he runs away from London; sees off his persecutors, the ghastly Murdstone siblings; and then generously pays for his education and sets him up in the law.

Dickens turns her into a mothering aunt. She rechristens David as Trotwood Copperfield, thereby implying her maternal claim. The softer emotions do not easily penetrate her defenses, but what does crack through is sincere and heartfelt.

"You are my adopted child," she tells David. "Only be a loving child to me in my age, and bear with my whims and fancies." David duly reciprocates with all love and respect, and the novel rewards her with a happy, active old age—we last see her "fourscore years and more, but upright yet, and a steady walker of six miles at a stretch in winter."

Dickens doesn't otherwise show much interest in aunts. His own played an insignificant role in his life, and the only other notable example of the breed in his writing is Mr. F.'s Aunt, a minor if brilliantly vivid character in *Little Dorrit*, notable not for her auntliness but for her psychotic alienation. With her incapacity to relate normally to her surroundings or companions, she is clearly the victim of a form of some autistic disorder. Although her utterances have comic force, she is no more than a bizarre one-off in the history of aunts.

But Betsy Trotwood has a large progeny. There are literally hundreds of aunts in later-nineteenth- and twentieth-century English literature who share her characteristics of gruff, fearless good-eggery and staunch disdain of fashion and custom. They may seem stern and unyielding on the surface, but they have only to be scratched or tickled to soften. There's Aunt Stanbury in Anthony Trollope's *He Knew He Was Right*, for example. A wealthy and rigid spinster, she takes in her niece Dorothy and tries to matchmake her with the repellent Reverend Gibson. When this scheme fails, she adamantly and apparently irrationally refuses to allow Dorothy to marry her heir, the more agreeable Brooke Burgess, but eventually relents. Or Mrs. Touchett, Isabel Archer's aunt in Henry James's *The Portrait of a Lady*. Living a peripatetic existence in amicable separation from her banker husband, she is "a person of many oddities . . . who had her own way of doing all that she did. . . ." In important matters, however, she hits the nail on the head, and her opposition to Isabel's marriage to the sterile dilettante Gilbert Osmond is based on sound moral precepts.

In the twentieth century, as women were allowed more freedom to roam, such aunts become increasingly wayward and unaccountable. In 1955, Edward Everett Tanner III, writing under the pseudonym Patrick Dennis, had enjoyed a huge success in the United States with *Auntie Mame,* a light and partly autobiographical novel based on the author's experiences with his aunt Marion. The novel won further fame when it was turned into a play and film (both starring Rosalind Russell), then a musical (starring Angela Lansbury on Broadway, Lucille Ball in film).

The narrator is a ten-year-old orphan, sent to New York from a respectable suburb of Chicago under the terms of his father's will, where his auntie Mame, a rich Manhattan sophisticate, is to bring him up. The year is 1929; she receives the boy in her bedroom, "wearing her bed jacket of pink ostrich feathers. She was reading Gide's *Les Faux-monnayeurs* and smoking Melachrino cigarettes through a long amber holder." Auntie Mame teaches Patrick worldliness; one day, July 14, 1929, he writes, "featured such random terms as Bastille Day, Lesbian, Hotsy-Totsy Club, gang war, id, daiquiri—although I didn't spell it properly—relativity, free love, Oedipus complex—another one I misspelled—narcissistic, Biarritz, psychoneurotic, Schönberg and nymphomaniac." To educate him further, she sends him to "a school coeducational and completely revolutionary. All classes are held in the nude under ultra-violet ray." The experiment doesn't last long.

Yet Auntie Mame isn't just a chic comic turn:

> That her amazing personality would attract me, just as it had seduced thousands of others was a foregone conclusion . . . but that she should care for an insignificant, uninteresting boy of ten was a constant source of delight and mystification to me. Yet she did, and I always thought that for all of her popularity, her interests, her constant comings and goings, she was probably a little lonely too. Her critics have said that I was simply a new lump of clay for her to shape,

stretch, mould and pummel to her heart's content, and although it is true that Auntie Mame could never resist meddling with other people's lives, she still had a staunch, undependable dependability. For both of us, it was love. . . .

THE REAL AUNTIE MAME

Many famous actresses portrayed Auntie Mame onstage and screen, most famously Rosalind Russell, who played her for fifteen months on Broadway, and then in the film adaptation of the wildly successful play by Patrick Dennis based on his novel. Other actresses who once played the madcap aunt in various stage productions included Greer Garson, Beatrice Lillie, Constance Bennett, and Eve Arden.

However, because the author, Patrick Dennis, narrated the novel on which the play and movie were based, and because some of the character's traits were based loosely on his eccentric aunt Marion Tanner, many readers assumed, wrongly, that his fiction was fact. According to the biography *Uncle Mame: The Life of Patrick Dennis* by Eric Myers (St. Martin's Press, 2000), Tanner said: "I wrote in the first person, but it is all fictional." According to this book, Aunt Marion and Aunt Mame did share

Rosalind Russell in *Auntie Mame*

several characteristics in common, including that they both were Buffalo-born, flamboyant, eccentric free spirits; lived in town houses in Greenwich Village; worked for a while at Macy's department store in New York City; had brief acting careers; and were terrible at managing their finances, running through lots of money.

Most telling is this passage from the book:

> But Pat [Dennis] insisted that the only similarity between Auntie Mame and his aunt Marion was that they were both crazy. "Anyone with any sense would know who Auntie Mame really is," he once said, then pointed to himself.

AUNT AUGUSTA

Another late variant of the stereotype is Aunt Augusta, the central figure of *Travels with My Aunt*, a novel by Graham Greene, published in 1969, which was also turned into a play and film (with Maggie Smith)—though not yet a musical. Its theme is in outline the same as that of *Auntie Mame*, but with a twist—a dreary bank clerk called Henry Pulling is visited by his long-lost aunt on the day of his mother's funeral. She decides that Henry needs the stuffing knocked out of him. First she takes him on a smuggling trip to Istanbul on the Orient Express, then to South America, where Aunt Augusta pursues the love of her life, the nefarious Mr. Visconti.

For Henry, the relationship is an education in the wilder shores of life. Augusta, who admits that she has worked extensively as a high-class prostitute, tells him that the woman he thought was his mother, Angelica, hadn't actually given birth to him, but had merely covered up for her sister who hadn't wanted to marry the baby's father. On the book's penultimate page, Augusta's true relation to Henry is revealed: He calls her "Aunt Augusta" and she doesn't respond; then he calls her "Mother" and she does.

AUNT DAHLIA AND AUNT AGATHA

But without a doubt, the most vividly depicted aunts in the Trotwood tradition are P. G. Wodehouse's Dahlia and Agatha, who operate on the good aunt–bad aunt principle. Wodehouse was obsessed with aunts, partly because his own childhood had been so dominated by them. The son of a Hong Kong magistrate, he was sent back to England, like many colonials' children, at an early age and passed around his relatives during school vacations. For years at a time, he didn't see his parents at all. As temporary mother substitutes, he variously endured Aunt Julie, who had three lovely daughters; Aunt Nim, a portrait painter who lived in bohemian Chelsea; Aunt Mary, a domestic tyrant of a literary bent, who lived with Aunt Loulie and Aunt Anne near Bath; Aunt Lydia; Aunt Edith; Aunt Constance and Aunt Alice, rectors' wives; Aunt Jane; and Aunt Amy. The psyches of Wodehouse's contemporaries Saki and Rudyard Kipling were deeply scarred by being farmed out in similar fashion. But Wodehouse adored school and must have been saved by his irrepressible tendency to see the funny side.

On the whole, he is anti-aunt. In the short story "Jeeves Makes an Omelette," his alter ego Bertie Wooster describes his position on the subject:

> In these disturbed days in which we live, it has probably occurred to all thinking men that something drastic ought to be done about aunts. Speaking for myself, I have long felt that stones should be turned and avenues

explored with a view to putting a stopper on the relatives in question.

Elsewhere aunts are blamed for all ills and failures. "Behind every poor innocent blighter who is going down for the third time in the soup," he moans, "you will find, if you look carefully enough, the aunt who shoved him into it. . . . If I had my life to live again, Jeeves, I would start it as an orphan without any aunts. Don't they put aunts in Turkey in sacks and drop them in the Bosphorus?" Aunts become the stuff of nightmares—"As far as the eye could reach I found myself gazing on a surging sea of aunts. There were tall aunts, short aunts, stout aunts, thin aunts and an aunt who was carrying on a conversation in a low voice to which nobody appeared to be paying the slightest attention."

Agatha and Dahlia are sisters to Bertie's father. Agatha, according to Bertie in *The Mating Season*, "is the one who chews broken bottles and kills rats with her teeth." She has "an eye like a man-eating fish" and "wears barbed wire next to the skin." Agatha reciprocates this low opinion, telling Bertie firmly that he is "an idiot" and objecting to what she sees as Jeeves's malignly protective influence.

Dahlia is something else. She is fond of Bertie in an exasperated way, greeting him with an affectionate "Hello, ugly," to which he responds by calling her "the old flesh and b" and, in rare sentimental moments, "my good and deserving aunt." Formerly an enthusiastic hunter, she retains a brick-red complexion and formidable strength. When her passions are roused, "strong men climb trees and pull them up after them," and at one point she knocks someone out with a thick, heavy stick. She has another crucial virtue: that of respecting Jeeves and his knack for hauling Bertie out of scrapes.

THEATRICAL AUNTS

The Aunt Agatha–Aunt Dahlia axis had long been the stuff of theatrical farce when Wodehouse created these two *monstres sacrés* in the 1930s. Plays about crotchety old maids who might leave their nieces and nephews some money, but have rigid views as to whom they should or shouldn't marry, were common currency throughout the nineteenth century. But the only two of these theatrical aunts who are remembered today appear in Brandon Thomas's *Charley's Aunt* (1892) and Oscar Wilde's *The Importance of Being Earnest* (1895).

Charley's Aunt is an astonishingly successful play that ran for four years after its London premiere and, according to *The Oxford Companion to the Theatre*, was once performed "on the same day in 48 different theatres in 22 languages, including Afrikaans, Chinese, Esperanto, Gaelic, Russian and Zulu."

Charley is a Bertie Wooster sort of undergraduate at St. Olde's College, Oxford, who is expecting a visit from Donna Lucia, his elderly widowed aunt just returned from Brazil, "where the nuts come from." Charley and his pal Jack are in love with two innocent young ladies but can't repectably entertain them in their rooms unless their guests are chaperoned. The chaps decide that Charley's aunt can serve that purpose and the girls are duly invited. To complete the party, they invite another asinine undergraduate who can entertain the aunt, leaving Jack and Charley to spoon the girls. Jack also invites his father, who is in financial embarrassment and could usefully marry Donna Lucia.

All these well-laid plans are thrown into disarray when Donna Lucia cancels at the last minute. The farrago eventually resolves itself with the right number of appropriate marital pairings.

Wilde's *The Importance of Being Earnest* is a play of classical formal perfection. Here the aunt is called Augusta, otherwise known as Lady Bracknell, and she belongs to the men-around-town Algy Moncrieff and Jack Worthing. She must rank as the nastiest aunt in English literature, and one of the nastiest mothers as well. She represents a new mutation of the British aristocracy that has eliminated noblesse oblige and substituted ruthless self-interest: For all her hauteur, she is ironically the most vulgar character in the play, being shamelessly materialistic and cynical in her values and attitudes. Traditionally, even the starchiest aunts melt a little at the sight of young love, but Lady Bracknell has no atom of sentimentality and in the last seconds of the play can only accuse her nephew Jack of "signs of triviality" when he throws his arms around his beloved Gwendolen and cries "At last!"

Was it the success of these two plays that fired a new vogue for comedies about aunts in the early twentieth century? The British Library catalog records at least fifty from this era, many of them designed for amateur performance. Although they continue to focus on the themes of inherited money and the suitable marriage partner for a niece or nephew, they follow other plot lines as well.

Aunts no longer command much interest in the theater these days, but they won't quite lie down and die. In 2004, an off-Broadway theater presented a new play by Miriam Jensen Hendrix called *When Aunt Daphne Went Nude*, a quaint nostalgic pastiche with a twist. It's 1934, and Reginald Walmesley, rising star of the Foreign Office, wants to marry Emily, a sweet girl from Vermont. Among the factors preventing the match are Emily's aunt, Millicent, who controls her money, and the anti-Semitic Daphne, who thinks Adolf Hitler is a darling and strips in the name of Nazi naturism and the body beautiful. It ran, not surprisingly, for less than a month and has not been heard of since.

REAL-LIFE ECCENTRICS

So much for fiction. Memoirs of the Victorian and Edwardian period are rich in real aunts as well. Among the most endearing is Aunt Etty, in Gwen Raverat's delightful memoir of her Cambridge childhood, *Period Piece*. Born in 1843, Etty was the eldest daughter of Charles Darwin, and although she was married and survived to a great age, her life was one of unimaginable supine idleness: "She told me, when she was eighty-six, that she had never made a pot of tea in her life; and that she had never in all her days been out in the dark alone, not even in a cab; and I don't believe she had ever traveled by train without a maid."

She was one of those Victorian lady valetudinarians who remained invalid all their lives with an illness or condition that is never specified or diagnosed. When she was thirteen and suffering from "a low fever," the doctor recommended that she have breakfast in bed for a time. The result was that "she never got up to breakfast again in all her life." Her ill health became "her profession and absorbing interest."

Nevertheless her nieces and nephews adored her—"to us she only showed her immense interest in everything in the world, her vitality, her affection." And despite her frailty, Etty was a woman of passionate convictions and a taste for controversy.

EXOTIC AUNTS

Another breed of aunts in this era was not so much eccentric as exotic—these were the ones who got away, the ones who broke the rules and did not opt for safety and respectability, thus sustaining an aura of adventure and romance about them. Cecil Beaton describes one such in his autobiographical *My Bolivian Aunt*. In connection with a speculation, the Bolivian entrepreneur Pedro Suarez visited the Westmorland home of Beaton's maternal family in the early 1890s and fell in love with Cecil's aunt Jessie. Although Suarez was public school educated and had top-drawer connections, the romance caused a great scandal—one thinks of poor Lilia Herriton in E. M. Forster's *Where*

Angels Fear to Tread—and once they were married, they headed back to South America, leaving Jessie's reputation in the Lake District tarnished if not disgraced.

Most startling of all were Jessie's clothes. Eschewing the "soft pale tints of the sweet pea" that the Edwardians considered pretty and decorous, she went for outright brilliance, crowning her outfits with hats that were "gigantic cartwheels with tall crowns from which sprouted a firework display of osprey, birds of paradise or huge funeral ostrich plumes." (These remained filed in Beaton's mind until they reemerged fifty years later when he was designing *My Fair Lady*.)

But all this wonderful gaiety and energy concealed her unhappiness at her husband's persistent infidelities. The couple returned to Bolivia, but eventually, at the end of her tether, she returned to England without him, claiming that she had been widowed. In a small flat in Maida Vale, she continued to be merry, dining off what was then an unimaginably bizarre cuisine of *arroz a la Valenciana*, *empanadas*, *churros*, *membrillo*, and *masaco*, as well as gamely posing in the remnants of her South American finery for her nephew's first photographic portraits. As she became poorer, she grew correspondingly more resourceful; her spirit was undaunted even by the excruciating cancer of the jaw that killed her. She emanated, writes Beaton in tribute, "a warmer atmosphere of love and friendship than almost any human being I have known."

NOTORIOUS AUNT BESS

Thomas Hinds, a writer and publishing consultant, lives in Tarrytown, New York, with his wife and teenage sons. He fondly remembers his great-aunt Bess, who had a far more colorful history than he ever knew as a boy, when she was one of his favorite babysitters:

My sister and I thought we knew Aunt Bess well. She was cool, she was funny, she never swore except when she was sewing, she had a fast and edged tongue and a raunchy sense of humor. She dressed well and drove strange, foreign cars—a Renault Dauphine in the early '60s. She sold liquor and had boyfriends, but no husband. From the late 1940s to the early '80s, she was a very active member of our family.

My mom trusted her implicitly, and left my sister, my brother, and I in her care even when we were babies. Although she lived in

Minneapolis and we lived some forty miles south, we saw her often, and she showed up for Christmas Eve and for all christenings and confirmations. When our parents went away on weekend trips, she babysat for us. She later babysat for my sister's children. She was our great-aunt, my grandfather's sister, and lived from 1898 to 1983.

One Easter Sunday in Northfield, Minnesota, 1954, my sister and I didn't pay much attention to the religious significance of the day. We were celebrating being left at home with Aunt Bess while my father and mother went away for a week.

Aunt Bess arrived after the Easter service was over. She didn't go to church. She brought in wine and whiskey although a dry Easter was more befitting of the Lutheran tradition in which we were being raised. She was wearing a gray sheared lamb coat, a cute black hat, and driving a flashy new Pontiac. Her hair was very auburn for a woman who was fifty-six. She was heavenly, and the opposite of the morning's sermon.

As kids, we thought we knew Aunt Bess well. Here are some of the interesting things we found out about her after her death:

- *Aunt Bess was the mistress of John Dillinger's "jug marker," Eddie Green, the guy who cased the banks. Eddie was shot down in front of her in an FBI ambush. She spent a year and a day in the Federal Women's Prison, Alderson, West Virginia, for harboring Dillinger. Her defense lawyer was Harold Stassen, perennial presidential candidate. Thomas J. Dodd, then FBI, later Connecticut senator, worked on her case guided by Melvin Purvis, the most famous of G-men under Hoover. Hoover followed the details of her case.*

- *We never knew her as "Beth Green," although the FBI did. In police custody, Aunt Bess, alias Beth Green, informed to the FBI. She enabled them to identify Dillinger's gang (and to capture or kill all members), to break up the Barker-Karpis gang, and capture the kidnappers of two local beer scions. She provided other information that helped to ensure the cleanup of wild St. Paul.*
- *In 1928, she was neighbor to her boss and protector, "Dapper Danny" Hogan, a capo of the St. Paul mob, when Danny was blown to glory as he stepped on the starter of his car. At that time, she was living with a runner for the biggest bootlegger in St. Paul. She also worked in, owned, or managed several notorious gangster hangouts and nightclubs in St. Paul from 1925 to 1934. She was then, and remained, close to Aunt Grace Rosenthal, a famous St. Paul madame.*
- *She continued as a "hostess" after she got out of prison until the early 1950s, skirting the edges of legality.*

Aunt Bess had chosen to live an unconventional life. Born in the last days of the Wild West, she lived for fifty years with few boundaries except, briefly, prison.

Her family loved her and she loved us back. Every year from 1928 to 1933, this woman, no matter what name she was using, had professional photographers take her picture. She would send a portrait-size copy to her relatives so that they could look at how well she was doing. Beth Green/Aunt Bess still deserves to be looked at; in fact, Bess would have loved the attention.

7

DAMNED BAD AUNTS

"To be sure, aunts of all kinds are damned bad things," complains Tony Lumpkin in Oliver Goldsmith's comedy *She Stoops to Conquer* (1773). P. G. Wodehouse's Bertie Wooster (see page 127) would have fervently agreed. Both fellows are, of course, great boobies, prize chumps, and laughingstocks. This book prefers to present aunts in a positive light, as beacons of a civilizing loving-kindness, at one remove from the intensely emotional power struggle that underlies parenthood.

But we must not sentimentalize: Tony's and Bertie's viewpoint must be given its due. There are aunts—of all kinds, at all times, in all places—who are indeed damned bad things.

VILLAINS

Look to the Victorian novel, that great treasury of human nature, for examples. The villain of Charlotte Brontë's *Jane Eyre* is Mrs. Reed, the heroine's aunt by marriage. Jane is an orphan, taken into the Reed family by her kindly uncle. After his death, Jane is left and demoted to Cinderella status. Being of a stubborn, passionate nature, Jane cannot bear to call her persecutor *aunt*—she remains Mrs. Reed, a barrier to life and love. "I am not your dear," Jane snaps, when a brief phony show of auntly affection is made. "Send me to school soon, Mrs. Reed, for I hate to live here."

Later in the novel, Mrs. Reed turns out to have been actively malign. When Jane's rich uncle in Madeira writes to offer to adopt her, Mrs. Reed tells him that Jane died in the typhus epidemic that swept through Lowood Institution, the hideous boarding school where Jane was confined. This is not just blind spite—Mrs. Reed hopes that her children will then inherit John Eyre's fortune. Her comeuppance arrives when her son runs to the bad and she is left to endure a lingering deathbed. Finding her laid so low, Jane's impulse is to forgive, but Mrs. Reed will have none of it and she dies unreconciled.

Elizabeth Barrett Browning's excessively melodramatic and

episodic verse novel *Aurora Leigh* was published in 1856, nine years after *Jane Eyre,* and shows lineaments of its influence. On the death of her hot-blooded Italian mother, the spirited black-eyed Aurora is sent to live with her all-too-English aunt.

She embodies the aunt as desiccated spinster, siphoning what could have been her natural affections into what Barrett Browning calls "a sort of cage-bird life . . ." She attempts to drill her niece into following suit, but like Jane Eyre, Aurora gets away, eventually marrying a man blind since his house burned down.

Not all auntly clutches are escaped. Linda Tressel, the eponymous heroine of Anthony Trollope's little-read novella published anonymously in 1867, has no such luck. Like Jane, she is an orphan. Her aunt Charlotte, with whom she lives in Nuremberg, is a fanatical Baptist, determined that her niece will marry her lodger, a dreary and conventional middle-aged clerk. Other Trollope novels—*He Knew He Was Right,* for example—show auntly meddling in marital matters eventually being quashed, but in this bleak tale Linda escapes with a younger man of her choice only to discover that he is a political insurrectionary wanted by the police. Shamed and cowed, Linda is forced to return to her aunt, and we are left to imagine the rest of their life together.

More subtle is the baneful auntly influence in Henry James's *The Wings of the Dove* (1902), where money rather than morality is the motor. Kate Croy's mother has died, and she is left with only her pathetic, disgraced, faintly sinister father, who lives in reduced circumstances. Kate's rich aunt Maud makes it clear that she will leave the girl her fortune, on the condition that she break with her father and the man she loves, a mere journalist, to marry somebody socially grand. Like Oscar Wilde's Lady Bracknell, Aunt Maud has a formidable imperiousness that brooks no opposition; she is entirely materialistic, but no fool.

DOUBLE TROUBLE

The force of one aunt is as nothing, however, against the power of two or more—the gaggle of aunts, pincer-clawed or with tentacles. Today such an image immediately evokes two cartoon figures: Bart Simpson's dreadful pair of aunts, sisters to his mother, the amiable downtrodden Marge. The cynical chain-smoking Selma Bouvier loathes her brother-in-law Homer implacably, but there may be an element of jealousy in this—her own two marriages ended in failure. Sideshow Bob had served time in jail for his attempt to frame Krusty the Clown before he tried to blow Selma up on their honeymoon. She then moved on to a two-bit movie actor Troy McClure, whom she married after his involvement in a scandal involving underage fish. Their union did not last long, and Selma now devotes herself to Jub Jub, her pet iguana. Patty Bouvier, another chain-smoker, is simply a vacuum whose job is administering eye tests for the Springfield Department of Motor Vehicles. To Bart and his sister Lisa, aunts represent nothing but trouble.

They would have sympathized with Hector and Ethel Munro. Some 120 years before *The Simpsons*, these real-life siblings were sent to live with their aunts Charlotte, known as Tom, and Augusta in North Devon while their father served in the military police in Burma. Their house was fetid, as the aunts mistrusted fresh air, and the atmosphere was further poisoned by the two women's mutual loathing and ceaseless bickering. Ethel recalls that Aunt Tom had "no scruples" and "never saw when she was hurting people's feelings . . . she was a colossal humbug and never knew it." The hypochondriac Aunt Augusta, meantime, had "a talent for being able to work herself into a passion over the most trivial annoyance."

What made young Hector's and Ethel's lives double misery was their aunts' feud, which extended to the boundaries of domestic discipline. "We could not obey both aunts," Ethel remembered. "I believe each gave us orders which she knew were contrary to those issued by the other." One forbade walking on grass; the other told them to keep off the gravel. Both were keen on religion, but neither of them "permitted it to come between her and her ruling passion, which was to outwit the other." What they squabbled about never seemed to be of much importance.

"We often longed for revenge," recalled Ethel, "with an intensity I suspect we inherited from our Highland ancestry"—and when they had escaped and grown up, Hector took it, deliciously so. Under the nom de plume of Saki, he became the author of very short, very bitchy stories with a sting in their tail, filling them with ludicrously stupid and unpleasant aunts, many of whom meet terrible ends or reversals of fortune.

George Eliot remembered her gaggle of maternal aunts with a little more affectionate understanding when she painted their group portrait in the drily amusing sixth chapter of her novel *The Mill on the Floss*, set in the rural Midlands among the lower middle class. The four Dodson sisters grew up with a high sense of their own respectability—"there was in this family a peculiar tradition as to what was the right thing in household management and social demeanor, and the only bitter circumstance attending this superiority was a painful inability to approve the condiments or the conduct of families ungoverned by the Dodson tradition." But within this squadron, the two daughters who had married "up" lord it over the two sisters who had remained merely respectable—and when the four sisters gather en masse for an Easter lunch at the mill, their children rebel in the face of a textbook demonstration of how aunts should *not* behave.

For all their shortcomings, the Dodson sisters are solidly rooted in reality; they are married, have children, and function as ordinary members of society. Spinster sisters tend to live together and turn inward, losing their grip on their sanity—not so much damned bad aunts as damned mad aunts, consumed by rituals and obsessions.

Brian Friel's play *Dancing at Lughnasa,* set in rural Donegal in the 1930s, is a poignant tribute to his unmarried mother and four aunts, whose only escape from drudgery and disappointment is a collective explosion of Dionysian revelry inspired by songs broadcast on the wireless.

VICTIMS

Damned bad, damned mad, or maybe simply damned—aunts are not so much predators as victims, the object of a desire for their money that leads its potential heirs to extreme measures. The theme was a staple of mid-twentieth-century crime fiction, stylishly twisted in Richard Hull's *The Murder of My Aunt* (1934), in which the narrator, forced to live alone with his stingy aunt in dreary rural seclusion, records in his diary his development of a fail-safe scheme to kill her by arranging for her car to crash. The surprise comes when the aunt suddenly takes over the story: It turns out that she has been reading her nephew's diary and tracking his every move, so she has dispatched him with an even nastier plot of her own. The joke of the prim maiden aunt who turns out to be a ruthless murderer is also played in Joseph Kesselring's play and film *Arsenic and Old Lace* (1944) and John Newton Chance's *Aunt Miranda's Murder* (1951).

But these fictions seem very tame compared with the appalling real-life aunt-murder stories that pepper newspapers all over the world. In a suburb of Chicago, James Zoph, thirty-seven, battered his frail and disabled aunt Wanda to death in 2004, her face marked by the imprint of his shoes. Zoph's only defense was that he felt he had been cheated out of a thousand-dollar inheritance. In Sydney, twenty-year-old Richard Cleverly strangled his forty-two-year-old aunt Susan to death in 2002 in the expectation of inheriting money she had left him in her will. In Kentucky, the corpse of Ann Branson, eighty-five, was discovered brutally stabbed and bludgeoned in 2003. An astute and successful businesswoman with a portfolio of rental properties, she had been lending her sweet-talking nephew Russell Winstead, a compulsive gambler, substantial amounts of money. Two days before her death, her ledgers recorded that she had received a check from Winstead reimbursing her for twelve thousand dollars. Ann's records, according to the *America's Most Wanted* Web site, "showed that she intended to deposit that check on Monday when the banks reopened. Cops say that if Ann had lived to deposit that check it would have bounced as high as a kangaroo in a moon bounce. As it was, the check was nowhere to be found." Winstead served as a pallbearer at her funeral; two years later, he was arrested in Costa Rica, and at the time of this writing awaits trial.

The *Guardian* of August 26, 2004, carried an interview with Susan May, then sixty, who was convicted in 1992 of the murder of her blind eighty-nine-year-old aunt Hilda. May had lived her entire life in a village in Lancashire. When her mother and aunt became elderly, she gave up her hairdressing salon to care for them, visiting her aunt several times a day to cook and clean and attend to her needs. Hilda was good-natured and cheerful, and nobody knew of any animosity between them. One morning, May arrived to find her aunt dead in bed, having been severely battered. Cupboard doors had been opened, but nothing appeared to be missing. Everyone's assumption was that she had died as the result of attack by a burglar, and May readily cooperated with the detectives, explaining that as a result of her daily visits and cleaning, her fingerprints would appear all over the house.

Her subsequent arrest left her so incredulous that she engaged only a local lawyer who had never represented someone accused of murder and who called only two defense witnesses against the prosecution's sixty. May was found guilty on the strength of evidence linking her fingerprints to what appeared to be a trace of her aunt's blood, and village gossip that her motive may have been need to get hold of her aunt's money in order to buy expensive gifts for her "toyboy" lover. May denies this, pointing out that her aunt was always openly generous with money, and there would have been no need to resort to murder—least of all on her mother's birthday.

After two appeals failed, the forensic evidence was called into severe doubt by researchers. In April 2005, Susan May was released from prison; she is now fighting on to clear her name.

8

LITERARY AUNTS

"My own darling child" is what Jane Austen called *Pride and Prejudice*. Women writers often bless their work with this biological existence, comparing the production of fiction to the painful ecstasy of childbirth, and in many cases the creating of lives through the written word provides a satisfying substitute for the impulse of maternity—the difference being that once a novel has been published, it requires no further nurturing and must be left to find its own way in the world.

So the woman writer may be left with a space in her emotional life that aunthood can neatly fill. Her literary imagination should bless her with the sympathetic ability to enter into the minds of her nephews and nieces, to understand them as independent beings and not merely extensions of their parents. She can also introduce them to her own inner storehouse of thoughts, fantasies, and tales, making her a source of wonderment. These were gifts abundantly held by the physically childless Jane Austen and Virginia Woolf—both great novelists and exemplary aunts.

AUNT JANE

Family was Jane Austen's primary interest. She remained with her parents—her mother outlived her by ten years—throughout her life, intimately affiliated to her seven siblings and their twenty-three offspring. They made that unfashionable thing, a functional family. In the words of biographer Claire Tomalin, the Austen children "grew up tough, not given to self-pity and notable for their mutual affection and support." There were tensions but no feuds, anxieties but no neuroses, and they were free of the intense introspection that made another literary family, the Brontës, so inept at forming outside attachments.

This warmth of feeling toward the family is reflected in Jane Austen's novels. Perhaps *tribal* is the best word to describe their sociology: They weave the threads of compatible dynasties into tapestries, excluding outright exogamy (the tall, dark stranger from nowhere holds no appeal) but accommodating cousins, stepparents, and second wives. The important thing is to fit in somewhere, with someone else. Marriage doesn't represent an assertion of independence or escape from the status of child so much as an extension of loyalty—the grafting of a new branch on to an ever-growing tree.

Jane Austen regarded her own aunthood with something like pride. When her niece Caroline became a very young aunt, Jane wrote to her: "Now that you have become an Aunt, you are a person of some consequence & must excite great Interest whatever you do. I have always maintained the importance of aunts as much as possible, & I am sure of your doing the same now." This wasn't an ironic joke: In several of her novels, the relationship between aunt and niece is shown as stronger, for both good and ill, than that between mother and daughter.

Yet none of Jane Austen's own aunts was of any emotional significance to her. Her mother's sister Jane died when Austen was eight. One of her father's sisters, Leonora, lived obscurely on charity somewhere, and was never mentioned. Her father's other sister, Philadelphia, was a dubious character, the widow of a surgeon based in India and apparently the mistress of the celebrated governor of Bengal, Warren Hastings. Although clearly a figure of great interest to the Austen household, she was known largely by letter and repute, as she went to live in France after the death of her husband, mixing in aristocratic circles.

It was Philadelphia's daughter Eliza who captured the young Jane's imagination, not her middle-aged aunt. Cousin Eliza, fourteen years Jane's senior, married Jean-François Capot de Feuillide, a dashing captain in Marie Antoinette's dragoons. Gay, flirtatious, and insouciant, Eliza adored balls, smart company, amateur theatricals—did Jane record her traits in the figure of Mary Crawford in *Mansfield Park*?—and on her visits to England, Jane was dazzled by Eliza's urbanity. In 1794, de Feuillide was guillotined; some twenty years later, Eliza married one of Jane's brothers, the wayward charmer Henry.

Jane had another pseudo-aunt in Anne Lefroy, a close neighbor blessed with an expertise in English literature who encouraged Jane in her early writing. It was with Mrs. Lefroy's nephew Tom that Jane conducted a flirtation that might have turned into something more serious had he not been sent off to train for the bar. The movie *Becoming Jane* fictionalizes this episode. Two years later, Mrs. Lefroy was the conduit to another abortive romantic incident when she introduced Jane to one Samuel Blackhall, a pompous Cambridge don who sounds rather like Mr. Collins in *Pride and Prejudice*. Jane was amused, but not interested.

By the time Jane died, her family had suffered financial reversals and Jane had nothing to leave her own nieces and nephews, but they had cause to remember her fondly: She had been a splendid aunt to all of them. Her niece Caroline later recalled how as "a very little girl, I was always creeping up to her and following her whenever I could . . . she would tell us the most delightful stories chiefly of Fairyland, and her fairies all had characters of their own—the tale was invented, I am sure, at the moment, and was sometimes continued for 2 or 3 days, if occasion served." Her niece Anna remembered the same magic: "Aunt Jane was the general favorite with children, her ways with them being so playful & her long circumstantial stories so delightful! These were continued from time to time, & begged for of course at all possible or impossible occasions, woven, as she proceeded, out of nothing, but her own happy talent for invention."

Perhaps Jane's finest auntly hour came in 1808 when her brother Edward's wife died after her eleventh confinement, and she took in her orphaned nephews, Edward, fourteen, and George, thirteen. Her niece Marianne remembered another occasion when her aunt was closeted in a bedroom with her elder sister Fanny, and she and Lizzy had heard "peals of laughter through the door, and thought it very hard that we should be shut out from what was so delightful." Was she reciting choice passages from *Pride and Prejudice*? Marianne left another vivid impression of the hilarity, exuberance, and fantasy that made her aunt so enchanting: She "would sit quietly working beside the fire in the library, saying nothing for a good while, and then would suddenly burst out laughing, jump up and run across the room to a table where pens and paper were lying, write something down and then come back to the fire and go on quietly working as before."

Her eldest niece, Fanny, seems to have been the favorite—at least, Jane described her as "almost another sister" and "could not have supposed that a niece would ever have been so much to me." Fanny was the daughter of Jane's third brother, Edward, and lost her mother when she was fourteen. Jane often stayed with her, accompanying her on her charitable visits to the poor and taking her to the dentist in London ("a disagreeable hour"). Most important were their long and "very snug" talks. Mature and self-possessed yet anxious, Fanny suffered in love, embroiling herself at the age of twenty with the earnest, evangelical John Plumptre and then panicking when the moment for commitment loomed.

Jane became her agony aunt. Should she advance or retrench? Mr. Plumptre was duly seen off and Jane and Fanny spent happy times together staying with another of Jane's brothers in

London, shopping and gossiping. With Anna, her eldest brother, James's, first daughter, Jane had another sort of relationship. She was more bright and beautiful than Fanny, but more highly strung and a handful, too. (It is significant that among the heroines of her aunt's novels, Anna loved Emma and "could not bear" Fanny Price, whereas Fanny's preferences were the opposite.) Anna wanted to write fiction, and rather than consulting her aunt on matters of the heart, she wanted help with her pen. That is what she got, in letters that provide fascinating insight into Jane Austen's own technique and taste.

Although she doesn't mince her views, she pays Anna the great compliment of taking her efforts seriously, as one practitioner, if not professional, to another. "We have been very much amused by your 3 books, but I have a good many criticisms to make—more than you will like," she begins one letter. She complains on the ground of mimesis and verisimilitude—things that were simply not like life; dislikes excessive descriptions ("you give too many particulars of right and left"); and notes inconsistency ("she seems to have changed her character"). A revelation about the past of another figure, St. Julian, "was quite a surprise to me; You had not very long known it yourself I suspect—but I have no objection to make to the circumstance—it is very well told—& his having been in love with the Aunt, gives Cecilia an additional interest with him. I like the Idea: a very proper compliment to an Aunt!—I rather imagine indeed that Nieces are seldom chosen but in compliment to some Aunt or other."

Anna did not prosper. Her husband, the Reverend Ben Lefroy, died young, leaving her with seven children, and they sank ever further into genteel poverty. Her literary aspirations fizzled out, though she published a short novel and two children's books, as well as making an aborted attempt to complete her aunt's unfinished comic masterpiece *Sanditon*.

Jane Austen must at some level have regarded her novels as her contribution to this family tree of births, deaths, and marriages. "As I very much wish to see your Jemima," she wrote to Anna after the birth of her first child, "I am sure you will like to see my Emma & have therefore great pleasure in sending it for your perusal." *Emma* was another of her own darling children: Would it also be fanciful to see the lineaments of her beloved nieces Fanny and Anna in its eponymous motherless heroine, "the Paragon of all that is Silly & Sensible, common-place & eccentric, Sad & Lively, Provoking & Interesting"—a girl of charm and imagination whose blunders stem from sheer adolescent willfulness and imperfect knowledge of herself? Emma could certainly do with an aunt to steady her, and perhaps that is the role assumed by her loving and sympathetic but candid and clear-eyed narrator.

Elizabeth Bennet in *Pride and Prejudice* needs no such careful handling. Mature beyond her years, she is robust in her values and attitudes to the point of pertness. Her problem is her parents—a stupid, shallow mother with hysterical tendencies, a cynical, cowardly father who avoids confrontation—and how best to get away from them. She needs to be treated like the adult that she is, and the only person who does so is her aunt Mrs. Gardiner—not her blood aunt, interestingly, but the wife of Mrs. Bennet's tradesman brother. She is "an amiable, intelligent, elegant woman," neither smart nor sophisticated, but thoroughly respectable and possessed of that peculiarly Austenian virtue, "candour" or plain speaking. In contrast to her quiet voice of middle-class reason booms the arrogance of Darcy's own monstrous aunt Lady Catherine de Burgh. She is nothing more than a caricature of entitled snobbish hauteur, but her utterances have a comic vitality that leaves thoroughly decent Mrs. Gardiner seeming merely pallid.

In Jane Austen's next novel, *Mansfield Park,* aunts are much more subtly and effectively contrasted. Fanny Price's parents are even more feckless than the Bennets (their nurturing of a child as timidly polite and conscientious as Fanny never rings true), and Fanny is willingly handed over to the not-so-tender care of her mother's sisters, Aunt Bertram and Aunt Norris. Aunt Bertram is a masterly study in female passivity. She is not unkind to Fanny and feels something like affection for her, based on her willingness to fetch and carry and play cribbage. Fanny reciprocates with dog-like devotion, not least because Aunt Bertram's patronage protects her from the bullying of Aunt Norris, herself a poor relation at Mansfield Park, sublimating her irritation at her status by lording it over an even poorer one.

The brusque ending to the novel has a fairy-tale quality: Aunt Norris gets her comeuppance, sent off to live in seclusion with the disgraced Maria "where their tempers became their mutual punishment," while the Cinderella figure of Fanny gets to marry her handsome (if pretty damned dull) prince Edmund and thereby becomes heir to the palace that is Mansfield Park. A final neat touch is the way that Fanny's younger sister Susan is brought on to take her place at Aunt Bertram's side ("the stationary niece—delighted to be so!") and is actually rather better at fulfilling the role than Fanny had been.

In *Persuasion,* the heroine has herself become the aunt. Anne Elliott is motherless but has an "auntie," not related by blood or marriage, in the elderly, reasonable Lady Russell (a portrait drawn from Jane Austen's pseudo-aunt Mrs. Lefroy?) in whom she can confide. At twenty-nine, Anne is relatively old to be unmarried, and she is resigned to her role of looking after her younger sister Mary's badly behaved children. This she is very good at ("you can always make little Charles do anything," Mary complains, "he always minds you at a word"), though it leads to the most violent instance of physical contact between human beings that any of Jane Austen's novels registers. Anne is nursing the sickly Charles when his two-year-old brother, Walter, leaps on to her back and clings indelibly to her neck until Captain Wentworth gently removes him—a gesture that bears a curious dream-like resonance, as though a deeper burden is being symbolically lifted from Anne's shoulders. Moments like these make *Persuasion*, the last novel that Jane Austen completed, wistful in tone, as if the author is privately fantasizing that there is still time for one of those missed opportunities to recur and redeem her from maiden aunthood.

But that was her fate, and it seems appropriate that it was a nephew, James Edward—the son of Jane's eldest brother, James—who should take the responsibility of writing her first biography. His portrait does her little justice, however. Published in 1870, it is varnished with a high-Victorian glaze of piety, discretion, and decorum that never suggests either the quick, boisterous, restless woman whose cynical intelligence sent shudders down the spines of the straitlaced, or the warm, funny, affectionate aunt who relished amateur dramatics, played catch with her nephews, and loved hearing about her nieces' boyfriends.

AUNT GINNY

The other notable aunt in the pantheon of English literature was also commemorated by her nephew: The first full biography of Virginia Woolf was written by Quentin Bell, younger son of her sister, Vanessa. An affectionate and even respectful work, it is nevertheless essentially different in style and intention from that of James Edward Austen-Leigh's. Alongside Michael Holroyd's *Lytton Strachey* and Leon Edel's *Bloomsbury: A House of Lions*, it stands as part of the first wave of writing about the Bloomsbury group, aimed at charting a network of intellectual and sexual relationships defiant of the blood-linked kinship in which Jane Austen was anchored.

Yet Virginia Woolf's parental family wasn't dissimilar from the Austens. Both were profoundly English, one might say, in their moral tone and mental structure—two large, broad clans of the upper middle class with a strong sense of social responsibility and a good sense of humor, articulate and literate in their philosophy, and neither extreme in their views nor extravagant in their behavior. In some imaginary meeting place outside history, they might have gotten along perfectly well. What separates them are the revolutions of the nineteenth century: the loss of confidence in the Church of England, the transformations wreaked by the railway, a nation that had become a democracy and seat of an empire, and a series of social changes that repressed more than they liberated. All of which made growing up female a far more complex and perilous business for Virginia Woolf than it had been for the robust Jane Austen.

Virginia Stephen was born in 1882, the daughter of the distinguished man of letters Sir Leslie Stephen and his wife, Julia. Both of them had been previously married, and the existence of children from these first unions made the dynamics of the cramped household extremely delicate: Leslie Stephen's daughter by Minny Thackeray was autistic, and Virginia was sexually molested by Julia's sons George and Gerald Duckworth. When Virginia was thirteen, her sad, beautiful, and aloof mother died, and her half sister Stella briefly assumed the maternal place before she herself died two years later. The tall, dark, narrow house they all inhabited in Hyde Park Gate, dominated by the presence of their morbidly work-obsessed paterfamilias, only added to the pall of deathliness.

Three aunts influenced this troubled, intense childhood. Virginia never knew her mother's aunt, the pioneering photographer Julia Margaret Cameron, who died three years before Virginia was born, but the family maintained vivid memories of the open-door bohemian lifestyle she pursued—a precursor to the easy sociability of Bloomsbury, it has been suggested. On the Stephen side were two aunts whose characters struck Virginia forcibly. Caroline Emelia was a fervent Quaker spinster and neurotic invalid who followed the gospel according to Florence Nightingale and devoted herself to charitable works. For Virginia, the fascination was her vivid talk, full of stories and moral examples. "All her life she has been listening to inner voices, and talking with spirits," wrote Virginia, "she is a kind of modern prophetess." (After Caroline Emelia died, Virginia wrote a memoir of her aunt—which unfortunately does not survive.) Anny, sister to Leslie Stephen's first wife, was a more vivacious personality, eccentric and absentminded, who wrote about her literary forebears (she was Thackeray's daughter and had known Charlotte Brontë and George Sand) with an unbuttoned idiosyncratic charm. All of them influenced the burgeoning consciousness of Virginia Stephen, that complex brew of dazzling genius and murky neurosis, intellectual clarity and emotional confusion.

In adulthood, she would mock quaint relics like Caroline Emelia as part of her rebellion against the Victorian tyranny of the family and the ethos that allowed a woman little choice in the matter of human relationships. She became openly defiant of her caste and its norms. For her husband she took an assimilated Jew, Leonard Woolf, in what soon became a sexless but loving partnership. Such libido as she had was channeled toward other women and the forbidden realm of sapphism. Fits of depression that sank into madness further intensified her alienation.

No wonder, then, that her fiction is rooted in a sense of human isolation. Jane Austen's novels always gravitate toward a consolidation of the bonds within families—a strengthening of the clan—but Virginia Woolf creates characters who seem to float around in the ether of their own thoughts, touching one another but never truly meeting or wholly communicating. Some of these figures may embody traits of her relations—Aunt Anny Ritchie feeds into the dippy Mrs. Hilbery in *Night and Day*, Mrs. Swithin in *Between the Acts* bears traces of the brooding Caroline Emelia—but they are dissociated from the familial web that governs *Emma* or *Mansfield Park*, and it is their "moments of being," their flashes of revelation, that validate them. Even in *To the Lighthouse*, where memories of her parents are revisited and their ghosts addressed, Virginia Woolf explores what separates people, not what unites them—Mrs. Ramsay, an image of her prematurely lost mother, sits at the dinner table with "a sense of being past everything, through everything, out of everything . . . as if there was an eddy—

there—and one could be in it, or one could be out of it, and she was out of it." She was "alone in the presence of her old antagonist, life."

Aunt Virginia and her niece Angelica

Yet Virginia always felt the potency of family, focusing her positive affections on her elder sister, Vanessa—a painter with a rollicking bohemian existence based in Charleston, a farmhouse on the Sussex Downs, where she was variously accompanied by her three children, an estranged husband (father to two of them), and an otherwise homosexual lover (father to the third). She and Virginia were locked into what Virginia described as a "close conspiracy," sometimes irritable but always intimate and devotedly loyal. Virginia idolized, or at least romanticized, her big sister—Vanessa in her eyes being the maturely stable and sensible Stephen, emotionally undemonstrative, secure in herself as a mother and lover, fertile in her womb, and easily productive as an artist. That she was in reality often horribly strained and anxious was something Virginia preferred not to notice.

In this blind adoration, there was inevitably a sprinkling of sibling rivalry, too. It could even seep into envy, as when Virginia reflected only half jokingly in her diary after looking at Vanessa's paintings that "You have the children, & the fame by rights belongs to me." Which would she have preferred? Although it may be hard to imagine the lean, acidulous, and generally neurasthenic Virginia as a doting domesticated parent, she did periodically nurse regrets about her childlessness.

However, by the time she was in her mid-forties, past the age at which she could have conceived, aunthood was happily providing her with a compensatory emotional satisfaction. "I scarcely want children of my own now," she wrote in 1927. "The insatiable desire to write something before I die, this ravaging sense of the shortness & feverishness of life, make me cling, like a man on a rock, to my one anchor. I don't like the physicalness of having children. . . ."

With that element removed, Vanessa's offspring, Julian, Quentin, and Angelica, could become "an immense source of pleasure" to Virginia. She hadn't much liked them as babies, partly because they consumed so much of Vanessa's precious attention, but as soon as they became characters, she adored them. Reared with twentieth-century freedoms that she had been denied, precociously relating to adults as their equals, they were "terrifyingly sophisticated . . . they have grown up without any opposition: nothing to twist or stunt. Hence they have reached stages at 16 or 17 which I reached only at 26 or 27." The distance between generations collapsed—"I can't believe that they're not my younger brothers," she remarked of Julian and Quentin. "It is very exciting the extreme potency of your Brats," she told Vanessa. "They might have been nincompoops—instead of bubbling and boiling and frizzling like so many pans of sausage on the fire." As their "poor dear dotty old aunt V" (a role she played up to the hilt), she would turn up the heat and gently cook them.

The most complex relationship was with Julian, the eldest. A big, clumsy, and forceful lad, he grew into "a vast fat powerful sweet tempered engaging young man into whose arms I let myself fall, half sister, half mother & half (but arithmetic denies this) the mocking stirring contemporary friend." She charted the subtle changes in their relationship with fascination ("Julian . . . is very queer; one finds him noticing and feeling, and taking up what last year was imperceptible to him"), but their bond was muddied by his literary bent, an invasion of her turf that made her uncomfortable. His first book of poems was published while he was still an undergraduate at Cambridge, and she was obscurely relieved at the tepid reception that it met. Later she wrote to him: "I don't see why you should worry yourself to write a novel. It's such a long gradual cold handed business. What I wish is that you'd invent some medium that's half poetry half play half novel . . . I don't see why with your odd assortment of gifts—philosophy, poetry, politics and some human interest, you shouldn't be the one to do it."

The undercurrent of disdain rose to the surface when Julian subsequently sent her an essay he had written on the art critic

Roger Fry, in the hope that she might take it on for the Hogarth Press, the imprint she and Leonard owned and managed. The risk misfired. Quite crisply, she rejected it—"you've not mastered the colloquial style. . . . so that it seemed to me . . . to be discursive, loose knit and uneasy in its familiarities and conventions." Julian was deeply wounded, and a coolness descended. Months later, she apologized, claiming a befuddled head. "I certainly didn't mean to say anything that could possibly hurt you. . . . Don't for God's sake let us quarrel about writing."

Quentin was more bumptious, less prickly—a plump, uproarious, good-time boy. At sixteen, so Virginia told Vanessa, "he came to lunch. That boy really is a marvel. He drank two full tumblers of strong Spanish wine, where I can only take a wine-glass; and it was a hot day; and then he went off to shop, and seemed quite as steady as usual, and came back to tea, and had a long argument with me about poetry and painting." Their conversation was knockabout, yet intimate. "Oh to be Quentin and going to Rome!" she wrote to him when he was twenty and off on his travels. "But my dear child, do you know that in half a century there will be methods of circumventing these divisions of aunt and nephew. By attaching a small valve to something like a leech to the back of your neck, I shall tap all your sensations." (She was prescient of the cell phone.)

Three years later, when tuberculosis confined him to a sanatorium, she kept him buoyant with gossipy, malicious, and amusing letters, full of risqué jokes about virgins and queers. Over Julian's hot literary ambitions she sprinkled cold water; Quentin's, on the other hand, she fostered, pleading with him to give up the brush for the pen—"Think how many things are impossible in paint: giving pain to the Keynes', making fun of one's aunts, telling libidinous stories, making mischief." Eventually, he would take her advice.

The ravishingly beautiful Angelica, youngest of the three and the child of Vanessa's liaison with the homosexual Duncan Grant, was Virginia's Pixie or Pixerina. She cooed and fussed over her niece, pulling her into a secret fairy-tale world of elves and "witcherinas" as well as making embarrassing demands for kisses. "She is sensitive," Virginia observed, "minds being laughed at (as I do)." She certainly was: In her memoirs, Angelica recalls her aunt's behavior as more agonizing than entrancing. Her mother was generally withdrawn and said little; Virginia's petting was in contrast overwhelming, her manner "ingratiating, even abject, like some small animal trying to take what it knows is forbidden."

Yet there is no doubt that the children were as mesmerized by their strange aunt as she was by them. Aunt Ginny may have been "barmy" and "cracked," but she certainly wasn't boring. The temperature rose when she came into the picture, and the three of them loved to exchange reports of her latest volleys of loose cannon. "I saw Virginia for a moment," wrote Julian, "she only had time for one story and a mere handful of vicious remarks and to betray one important secret."

Then came tragedy, in what was perhaps the most shocking of all the premature deaths in Virginia Woolf's history. In March 1937, notwithstanding his family's pleas, Julian volunteered as an ambulance driver for the Republican cause in the Spanish Civil War. Four months later, he was killed, at age twenty-nine, by a shell. Everyone had known that the risk of such a catastrophe was high, but the family's response to the news was incredulous. Twelve days later, in an ache of melancholy and remorse, his stunned aunt very quickly wrote down "what I remember about Julian."

His "peculiar way of standing; his gestures were, as they say, characteristic. He made sharp quick movements, very sudden, considering how large and big he was, & oddly graceful. I remember his intent expression; seriously looking, I suppose at toast or eggs, through his spectacles."

The last time she saw him, sitting at the wheel of a car "frowning, looking very magnificent, in his shirt sleeves; with an expression as if he had made up his mind & were determined, though there was this obstacle—the car wouldn't start. Then suddenly it jerked off."

His "rather caustic teasing. He thought I wanted to give pain. He thought me cruel, as Clive [Julian's father] thinks me; but he told me . . . that he never doubted the warmth of my feelings; that I suffered a great deal: that I had very strong affections."

The "damned literary question," over which she is painfully honest. "I was always critical of his writing, partly I suspect from the usual generation jealousy; partly from my own enviousness of anyone who can do in writing what I can't do. . . . I thought him 'very careless,' not an artist, too personal in what he wrote, & 'all over the place.' This is the one thing I regret in our relationship: that I might have encouraged him more as a writer."

Most poignant and vivid of all is the painting of a little scene when the decision to leave for Spain was still unmade:

> I wanted him to stay. And then again I felt, he's afraid I shall try to persuade him not to go. So all I said was, Look here Julian, if you ever want a meal, you've only to ring us up. Yes he said rather doubtingly, as if we might be too

> busy. So I insisted. We can't see too much of you. And followed him into the hall, & put my arm round him & said You can't think how nice it is having you back [from China, where he had spent some time teaching] & we half kissed; & he looked pleased & said Do you feel that? And I said yes & it was as if he asked me to forgive him for all the worry; and then off he stumped in his great hat and thick coat.

A mother could have followed him; an aunt is left at the door, only half kissed.

9

FAIRY-TALE AUNTS

Until the eighteenth century, nobody gave their aunt a second thought—or at least that's the impression the written record leaves. Aunts don't figure with any potency or vividness in the Bible or classical mythologies. Stith Thompson's epic survey of the themes and motifs in folk cultures records only a few auntly appearances, and even those are peripheral or incidental. Bogeymen and stepmothers abound in children's stories, but there are no aunts of any significance in the fairy tales of Perrault, Grimm, or Hans Christian Andersen. On the subject of aunts, *The Oxford Dictionary of Nursery Rhymes* records only this riddle, dating from 1630:

There were three sisters in a hall
There came a knight amongst them all;

Good morrow, aunt, to the one,
Good morrow, aunt, to the other
Good morrow, gentlewoman, to the third,
If you were aunt,
As the other two be
I would say good morrow
Then, aunts, all three

This dearth of mythical aunts may surprise us, as aunts feature so prominently in modern children's literature that we have come to think of them as a basic ingredient of fantasy—specifically, of the phenomenon described by psychoanalysis as "the family romance," in which (according to Bruno Bettelheim) children are seized by

> the idea that one's parents are not really one's parents, but that one is the child of some exalted personage, and that, due to unfortunate circumstances, one has been reduced to living with these people, who claim to be one's parents. These daydreams take various forms; often only one parent is thought to be a false one—which parallels a frequent situation in fairy-tales, where one parent is the real one, the other a step-parent.

Yet for millennia, aunts somehow succeeded in sidestepping this Oedipal drama. Instead of replacing a mother, they supplement her: An aunt is a reassuring rather than disruptive figure, representing security and stability, patience and wisdom, reflective of the secondary meaning of the word *aunt* as any familiar and benevolent elderly lady in one's community. The literary function of aunts was to collect stories, rhymes, and homilies and provide disinterested advice on life.

Pompous nonsense is something that many evangelizing Christian lady authors spouted when they wrote improving books for the young. Describing themselves as Aunt such-and-such guaranteed a tone of friendly familiarity—taking the 1850s through the 1870s alone, the library catalogs list new pamphlets and tracts and anthologies by Aunt Agnes, Aunt Fanny, Aunt Louisa, Aunt Mary, and Aunt Mildred. Charlotte M. Yonge became Aunt Charlotte when she published her *Stories of English History*, *Evenings at Home with the Poets*, and *Scripture Readings;* and in the United States, Sarah Schoonmaker Baker took the pseudonym of Aunt Friendly for her pioneering teenage novels *The Boy Friend*, *The Children on the Plains*, and *The Jewish Twins*.

But about the same time that these books appeared, the aunt suddenly developed a more definite fictional personality of her own. To establish why this happened, you could delve deeply into the conflicting theories proposed by anthropologists, sociologists, and historians about the rise and fall, or the fall and rise, or the persistence or nonexistence, of the nuclear family and the extended family in industrial societies, but you would probably not resurface much enlightened. Perhaps it is better just to accept that the later Victorians found the notion of the bloodline aunt very interesting and amusing.

American children's literature of this period is almost obsessively interested in the sentimental theme of the orphan child sent

to live with an aunt. Literary critics trace this to the success of Elizabeth Wetherell's *The Wide, Wide World,* published in 1850, in which the ardent and impulsive thirteen-year-old Ellen gradually softens the heart of frosty, flinty, spick-and-span Aunt Fortune. The same situation recurs many times in books of the subsequent era—in Kate Douglas Wiggin's *Rebecca of Sunnybrook Farm,* for example, where the eponymous heroine is sent to live with "conscientious, economical, industrious" Aunt Miranda; or in Susan Coolidge's *What Katy Did,* where the "very neat and particular" Aunt Izzie finally reveals "a warm heart hidden under her fidgety ways"; or in Eleanor H. Porter's *Pollyanna* (1913), where a starchy spinster takes responsibility for her orphaned niece out of a sense of duty rather than affection, but finds herself ultimately disarmed by Pollyanna's "glad game" of finding "a silver lining in every cloud."

AUNT POLLY

Boys have aunts, too, notably Mark Twain's Tom Sawyer, whose Aunt Polly is powerless before his charm. "Laws-a-me!" she wails. "He's my own dead sister's boy, poor thing, and I ain't got the heart to lash him somehow." But she remains a flat, unexplored personality who plays no real part in the novel, similar to Dorothy's nondescript Auntie Em in L. Frank Baum's *The Wonderful Wizard of Oz*. More psychologically authentic is the relationship that Tom's friend, the genuine outsider Huckleberry Finn, doesn't have with the Widow Douglas: "She took me for her son," he tells the reader, "and allowed she would sivilize me; but it was rough living in the house all the time, considering how dismal regular and decent the widow was in all her ways; and so when I couldn't stand it any longer, I lit out."

THE MOVIE AUNT: CLARA BLANDICK AS AUNT POLLY AND AUNTIE EM

Dorothy in *The Wizard of Oz:* "Oh, but anyway, Toto, we're home. Home! And this is my room, and you're all here. And I'm not gonna leave here ever, ever again, because I love you all, and—oh, Auntie Em—there's no place like home."

In *The Wonderful Wizard of Oz*, and the other *Oz* books, Auntie Em, whose real name is Emily, is married to Uncle Henry, and the aunt of Dorothy Gale, who lives with them on a Kansas farm. Auntie Em was played in the movie by Clara

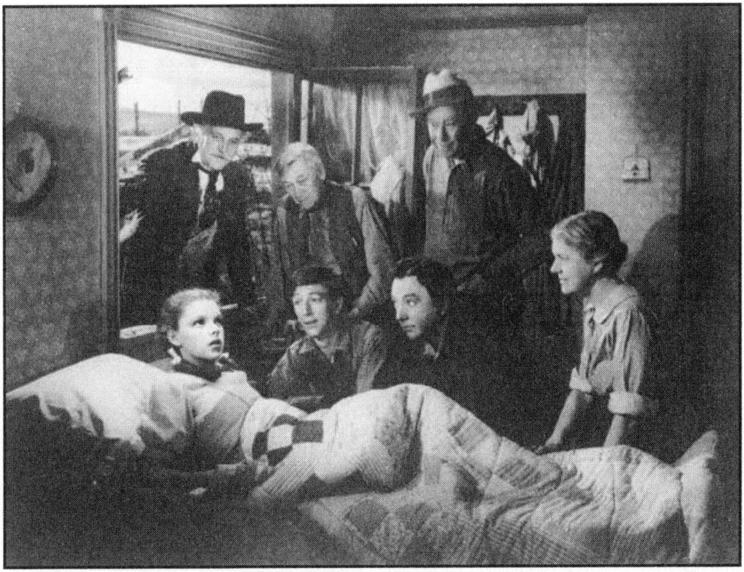

No place like home

Blandick (1880–1962). Her costume was simple: a housedress and apron. Unlike many of the other characters, Auntie Em did not have a counterpart in Oz. Perhaps this was because even in Dorothy's dream world, Auntie Em was too important a symbol of Dorothy's quest to return home to have a substitute.

Blandick, a character actress with a long movie career, was best known for her two roles as an aunt: Auntie Em in MGM's adaptation of L. Frank Baum's *Oz* books in 1939, and Aunt Polly in the 1930 movie version of *Tom Sawyer*. Blandick reprised her role as Aunt Polly in the 1931 film *Huckleberry Finn*.

In 1962, when she was eighty-one, after many years of illness, in pain, and losing her sight, she took her own life.

AUNT MARCH

Louisa May Alcott tried a bit harder. An enthusiastic aunt herself, she was much influenced in childhood by the stories told her by her own, rather grand great-aunt who had known Martha Washington and General Lafayette. Perhaps she contributed to the figure of the lame, grouchy, and wealthy Aunt March in *Little Women,* to whom Jo, Beth, Amy, and Meg, living in reduced circumstances, are unfortunately beholden in expectations of inheritance. A later and lesser-known novel of Alcott's, *Eight Cousins, or The Aunt-Hill,* presents Rose, yet another orphan who is taken in and fussed over by six maiden aunts, their personalities ranging from the pious and lugubrious Aunt Myra to the "truly beautiful old maiden" Aunt

Peace, "an adviser, confidante and friend." Although these ladies are sympathetically treated in the novel, it is the male influence of Uncle Alec, a sexy doctor, that helps Rose to grow up strong and sensible.

EVIL AUNTS

In twentieth-century children's literature, aunts learn to be callous and even hostile. Something very unpleasant happens to aunts when they are drawn into the violent and grotesque world of Roald Dahl. In *James and the Giant Peach* (1967), they become evil grotesques drawn on Cinderella's Ugly Sisters. James is orphaned after his parents are eaten by a rhinoceros, and he is sent to live with two "really horrible" aunts, Sponge and Spiker. Sponge is fat and short with piggy eyes, reminiscent of "a great white soggy over-boiled cabbage." Spiker is lean and tall and bony, with "a screeching voice and long wet narrow lips." They call innocent James "selfish and lazy and cruel" and "the disgusting little beast" and never let him out of their "queer ramshackle house." Each aunt, one fat and one thin, thinks she is the more beautiful one, as comically noted in a poem they speak as they admire themselves. Fortunately, the Giant Peach that rescues James from his incarceration rolls over them, leaving them ironed out flat, dead, and unredeemed.

These coarse caricatures are imitated by J. K. Rowling in her Harry Potter cycle. The orphaned Harry is lodged with his late mother's hysterical sister Aunt Petunia, a vicious termagant who bullies and humiliates Harry in favor of her fat and disagreeable son. Her husband, Vernon, has a sister, Aunt Marge, who comes to visit in *Harry Potter and the Prisoner of Azkaban.* "Huge, beefy and purple-faced," with a mustache and a bulldog, Marge is so pompous and infuriating that Harry illicitly draws on his magic powers to inflate her like a balloon and send her floating up to the ceiling.

ADOPTIVE AUNTS

Such revenge fantasies are not very edifying. They are enjoyed precisely because that's what they are, but the sad effect is to leave children regarding their aunts less as possible allies than as paper-tiger authority figures, waiting to be mocked and shot down. A more subtle and endearing treatment of auntly adoption is provided by Eva Ibbotson's *Island of the Aunts* (1999), a delightfully imaginative novel that takes the spite out of Dahlian excess. "Kidnapping children is not a good idea," runs its opening paragraph. "All the same, sometimes it has to be done." Etta, Coral, and Myrtle are aunts with only one deeply unsatisfactory niece and nephew. The three middle-aged ladies live on a desert island with their centenarian father and prophetic cousin Sybil. As eco-conscious guardians of the exotic fauna and flora, they are in need of fresh blood and help from open-minded youngsters—hence the kidnapping scheme.

They return to England to find suitable victims and invent an agency, Universal Aunts (see page 115). Aunt Etta, who does "fifty press-ups before breakfast" and has "a small but not at all unpleasant moustache on her upper lip," is sent to King's Cross station with the assignment of escorting Minette, an unhappy child who is being shuffled between neglectful divorced parents in London and Edinburgh. Arty Aunt Coral takes charge of Fabio, a half-English, half-Brazilian boy whose snobbish grandparents are sending him back to a boarding school he detests. Ditsy Aunt Myrtle mistakenly ends up with a spoiled American brat, Lambert.

The three children are whisked back to the desert island, where the aunts provide Minette and Fabio with an education in wonder.

They are put to work milking goats, feeding seals, and de-oiling birds, and they meet mermaids, dragons, and friendly monsters. Soon they grow to love the place, the aunts, and their labors; Lambert, however, just whines and plots his escape with the help of his dratted cell phone. The climax comes when the kraken wakes in the sea, transforming nature with his healing hum.

Back in London, the police are alerted to the disappearances, and newspaper headlines proclaim AUNT PLAGUE MENACES THE CITY. "There was talk in parliament of a curfew for aunts, forcing them to be in bed by eight o'clock; the *Daily Echo* said that aunts should be electronically tagged." Eventually, through Lambert's conniving, the children are "rescued" and the aunts charged with kidnapping. Aunt Myrtle escapes prosecution because Lambert's father is too lunatic and paranoid to press charges. In court, Minette and Fabio announce that Etta and Coral had chosen, not kidnapped, them; they were detained neither by force nor for ransom. The aunts are let off and bequeath the children the magic island in their will.

Etta, Coral, and Myrtle are typical of the modern aunt in children's books. They continue to represent a moral influence, but not one relating to everyday notions of good behavior—instead they are liberators, opening conventional childhoods to the adventure of eccentricity.

In Madeleine L'Engle's science-fiction quest novel *A Wrinkle in Time,* the paralyzed heroine Meg is nursed back to health on the planet Ixchel by Aunt Beast, a monster with tentacles and no hair or eyes, but the warmest of hearts. Paddington Bear's aunt Lucy pays for an inflatable dinghy with accumulated postal orders.

In an era in which a mass corporate culture cynically hard-sells children an ever-narrower range of options, products, and models, aunts such as these show the way to a simpler yet richer world that celebrates the freedom to be crazy but different—in other words, yourself.

SPIDER-MAN AND AUNT MAY

In the Marvel Comics Spider-Man series, created by writer Stan Lee and artist Steve Ditko, Peter Parker, who also leads a secret life as the superhero Spider-Man, has an aunt by marriage called Aunt May (Parker). Aunt May's first appearance was in Amazing Fantasy #15, which appeared in August 1962. Overprotective Aunt May—who along with her husband, Ben, takes in her nephew and raises him after the death of his parents—has no clue that her frail nephew is Spider-Man.

In the recent trilogy of *Spider-Man* movies, Aunt May is played by Rosemary Harris.

Tobey Maguire and Rosemary Harris in *Spider-Man 2*

10

HONORARY AUNTIES

Most of the aunts in this book are blood-related sisters of a parent, and it would be fair to generalize that they are the source of the most intense love that courses to or from a niece or nephew. A spousal aunt, to whom one is related only by an uncle's marriage, rarely provokes such emotion.

But there is another sort of aunt to consider, too, one with no place on the family tree: This is the *auntie*, in the sense specified by the *Oxford English Dictionary* as "a term of familiarity or respect applied to an elderly woman," almost synonymous with the Tudor English *goody* (short for *goodwife*) and applicable to just about any post-menopausal female who might otherwise be called ducky, dear, or love.

In Britain, it has historically been a word and a concept most widespread among the working class; the middle class has tended to be more particular about distinguishing an honorary auntie from a blood-related aunt, while the upper middle class generally eschews it altogether. It can also substitute for other familial titles; when I was a small child, the old lady whom everybody called Auntie Jo was in fact my great-grandmother—something that was never explained to me and left me very confused.

The *Oxford English Dictionary* qualifies its definition of *auntie* as something "applied esp. to a Negress." It has certainly long been a very popular expression in Afro-American culture. In *Uncle Tom's Cabin* (1852), for example, Uncle Tom's wife is called Aunt Chloe—she is, as Harriet Beecher Stowe puts it, "aunt to nobody in particular, but [an aunt] to human nature generally." (See also the discussion of Aunt Jemima Pancake Mix on page 104.)

The great majority of aunties are passing figures in the parade of life, so called only as a sort of courtesy title of no real emotional or even practical significance beyond the aura of benevolence they attract and emanate. "These aunties," writes Penney Hames in *The Daily Telegraph*, "were the sort you saw daily. The sort who lived only a hopscotch away, swapped Rice Krispie biscuit recipes with your mother, knew that you did swimming on a Wednesday and stay downstairs with a brandy and *The Generation Game* when your parents went out for the evening."

But aunties can be more than good neighbors by another name: They can also take on the roles and responsibilities of a blood aunt—surrogate aunts, you could call them. Typical of these was the novelist Winifred Holtby, who enjoyed an intense friendship and working partnership with the pacifist and feminist Vera Brittain dating back to their Oxford days. When Vera was swept up by the success of her First World War memoir *Testament of Youth* in the mid-1930s, it was Winifred who stepped in to look after her young children. Winifred, unmarried and childless herself, developed a relationship with little John and Shirley (later famous as the politician Shirley Williams) that was warmer and closer than the one they enjoyed with their formidable mother. "When Winifred was in charge," Shirley recalled forty years later, "my brother and I would pile up tons of cushions, and sit on top pretending to be maharajahs, or dress up in old bonnets and bowlers as fashionable Victorians." Winifred died tragically young, when Shirley was barely five, but her memory remained vivid.

A VERY MODERN AUNTIE EM

Emily Morgan, forty-nine, the personal manager of an athlete, of New York City, on being the godmother and honorary aunt to Timothy, age seven:

Before he was born, Timothy's mothers, who are close friends, approached me about being one of his godmothers. It was something we all took very seriously. They were asking me to be one of the adults in his life who would be responsible for him, who would help raise him. I felt honored to be asked. My partner and I don't have children. I don't have brothers or sisters, so I don't have any other nephews or nieces.

I was in the birthing room when Timothy was born, and I held him for four hours while his mothers got some rest. I bonded with him then. That was when our connection was formed, and he's been a joy ever since. That was when I became his Auntie Em.

I live cross-town from him and see him every month, sometimes more. For the past several years, he's had some sleepovers at my apartment. We go to the circus, to movies, shopping for toys, to the playground. I bought him his first bike. Last week we were at a restaurant and he ate three grilled cheese sandwiches, ordering one after the other. I take him to see Santa every year. It's all new to me and fun.

He's a smart, good kid, very literal. We talk about school and his mean teacher. He's in first grade. He likes everything to be right. If I say the title of a movie wrong, he corrects me.

I hope we remain close throughout his life. I'd like to travel with him when he's older. I just have him in small doses, which gives me a small window into being a parent. Being with a child helps give me perspective that life is about a lot more than just working late every night. When Timothy is with me, I spoil him. I let him stay up later than he's allowed to at home. That's my role.

AUNT DAN

Such aunties can be a profound influence on a child, perhaps because they stand at one remove from the family and its norms. Wallace Shawn's haunting play *Aunt Dan and Lemon* (1985) records this phenomenon in the case of a sensitive eleven-year-old girl known as Lemon (actually Leonora) who is in thrall to her parents' best friend, known as Aunt Dan. Aunt Dan is not conventionally benign. She is sexually omnivorous and a product of the liberations of the 1960s, who has ended up far to the right with an obsessive crush on Henry Kissinger. "There's something inside us that likes to kill," she insists.

Lemon's parents drop Dan, finding her politics too hot to handle, but Lemon is hypnotized by this weirdly charismatic woman and continues to see her well into her teens. At one point there is a frisson between them that suggests they might go to bed together, but it passes, and Aunt Dan dies when Lemon is nineteen. Lemon is left disturbed by Dan, with a respect for Nazism that she can't quite explain. At the end of the play, Lemon addresses the audience:

> Because if there's one thing I learned from Aunt Dan, I suppose you could say it was a kind of honesty. It's easy to say we should all be loving and sweet, but meanwhile we're enjoying a certain way of life—we're actually living—due to the existence of certain other people who are willing to take the job of killing on their own backs, and it's not a bad thing for everyone once in a while to admit that that's the way we're living, and even to give to those certain people a tiny, fractional crumb of thanks.

AUNT TID

An auntie can also be a foster parent. Edmund Kean, the great actor of the early nineteenth century, was brought up by Charlotte

Tidswell, a two-bit actress he called Aunt Tid, who had been mistress to both his uncle and the duke of Norfolk. Why did Aunt Tid endure him? As a child, he was so obstreperous and runaway that she had to tie a dog collar around his neck with the inscription BRING THIS BOY TO MISS TIDSWELL, 12 TAVISTOCK ROW. Was she compelled by some first intimation of his histrionic genius? Certainly he later paid tribute to her as the primary inspiration of his theatrical career, and their relationship would survive even Kean's self-destructive superstar capacity to fall out with anyone who'd ever helped, admired, or loved him. He acted at her final benefit performance in 1822, and ten years later she was there to nurse him in his pathetically washed-up dying days.

AUNTY SARAH

Rudyard Kipling recalls his aunty with unmitigated loathing in his autobiography *Something of Myself*. When he was seven, his itinerant parents parked him (while they were stationed in India) in what he describes as a "house of desolation" in Southsea. It was owned by a Mrs. Sarah Holloway, who had to be called Aunty. A domestic tyrant, her sadistic bullying and torturing went way beyond anything experienced by his contemporary Hector Munro, similarly dumped in Devon (see page 146). Kipling's bitterness at her treatment "drained" him, he thought, "of any capacity for real, personal hate for the rest of my days."

OPERATIC AUNTS

Only two blood aunts feature in the operatic repertory. One is the monstrous Zia Principessa, "Aunt Princess," in Puccini's *Suor Angelica*. The other is Brünnhilde in Wagner's *Der Ring des Nibelungen*. She really belongs in the chapter "X-Rated Aunts," as she is technically the lover of her nephew Siegfried, via her father Wotan, who is also father to Siegfried's parents, the twins Siegmund and Sieglinde. The incestuous nature of the latter's union is a bone of contention in the *Ring*'s second installment *Die Walküre*, but Wagner doesn't pursue it when it comes to Siegfried and *Brünnhilde* getting together in *Siegfried*.

AUNTIES AROUND THE WORLD

The auntie is a particularly potent figure in India, crossing several complex linguistic and cultural domains. Probal Dasgupta's study *The Otherness of English: India's Auntie Tongue* (1993) explores the auntie as "a significant fact in the domain of Indian English usage," quoting Kamal K. Sridhar's view that she "functions as a marker of Westernised sophistication among the upwardly mobile middle classes in urban and semi-urban India." In Indian English, it emerges, "middle and upper-middle class children who got to English-medium schools address their friends' mothers as Auntie." This cannot be new: In *The Raj Quartet,* Paul Scott's novels about the British withdrawal from India in the 1940s, the ingenuous Daphne Manners shyly asks whether she can call Lady Chatterjee auntie. Interestingly, *auntie* is also a common Indian slang term for "prostitute" or "madam." The *Oxford English Dictionary* doesn't record this usage after the seventeenth century, but it may have continued to have some oral currency in Britain—in Montagu Slater's libretto for Benjamin Britten's opera *Peter Grimes* (1945), set in Suffolk in the early nineteenth century, a woman known universally as Auntie runs a pub that doubles as a bawdy house, populated by her "nieces."

Auntie has many other euphemistic applications, all redolent of cozy comfort and moral rectitude. In the United States, it's the name of an anti-litter campaign and a firm selling politically progressive T-shirts bearing anti-Bush slogans. In New Zealand, the Aunties are the nation's "most innovative and loved family entertainers"; at Aston University, Aunties is the name of a scheme in which senior students befriend bewildered freshmen.

In the United States and Europe, the domestic use of the *auntie* honorific is now on the decline (except perhaps among pious Afro-Caribbeans). This can largely be ascribed to changes in social etiquette making it no longer impolite for a youngster to call an adult woman by her unadorned Christian name; too, *auntie* seems somewhat quaint, if not vaguely offensive, in its implication of prim propriety and middle age. In her *Daily Telegraph* article, Penney Hames concludes that "from a 21st century perspective, there's something about 'auntie' that reeks of an outdated and almost embarrassing preciousness and deference. As a child, I loved it, but as an adult, I squirm. Its passing is a sign of the times, much like wall-mounted tea caddies, Formica tabletops and Green Shield Stamps. We love their memory, but we don't want them back."

AUNTIE BEEB

The British Broadcasting Corporation was for many years nicknamed Auntie or Auntie Beeb. Nobody can trace the coiner of this jibe, but according to Asa Briggs's authoritative *History of Broadcasting in the United Kingdom*, it seems to date from the postwar years, when the BBC established a strict code of taste and decency that sought to lead the nation's ethical standards by example (perhaps not such a bad idea, one might think, in the era of *Big Brother* and worse). This wasn't just a matter of censoring steamy love scenes, but also involved a ban on the display of betting odds at the races and the satirical impersonation of politicians. Nowadays the press tends to wheel out the epithet only when a commentator wishes to mock the BBC's "commitment to public service broadcasting."

AGONY AUNTS

The most familiar manifestation of the auntie, however, is the agony aunt. An *agony aunt* has been defined by Wikipedia as "[a] columnist at a magazine or newspaper who writes a segment commonly known as an advice column. The image presented was originally of an older woman providing comforting advice and maternal wisdom, hence the name 'aunt.' . . . An agony aunt answers readers' queries on personal problems, in particular giving advice about sexual problems. In many cases, the queries, as well as the answers, have been created in the office, and the agony aunt is actually a team of writers. . . . The term is beginning to fall into disuse, as the scope of personal advice has broadened, to include overtly sexual matters—pioneered by the likes of Dr. Ruth [Westheimer]—as well as general lifestyle issues."

The practice of writing to "a lady" to seek advice on romantic quandaries goes back to the mid–eighteenth century, when a middle-aged ex-actress called Mrs. Eliza Haywood solicited let-

Dr. Ruth Westheimer

ters from the public in a short-lived journal called *The Female Spectator*.

Robin Kent's interesting history of this journalistic phenomenon can't locate the point at which such columnists became known as agony aunts, but she notes that the hero of P. G. Wodehouse's novel *Sam the Sudden*, published in 1925, takes a job as Aunt Isobel in *Pyke's Home Companion*, continuing a Victorian tradition of men crossing gender to become pseudonymous agony aunts. But by the 1950s, the agony aunt had become openly female, and advice was sought on the brave new world of sexual technique, open relationships, and chemical contraception.

11

THE GOOD AUNT GUIDE

DEAR AUNT MEF

Karen Washabau, fifty-nine, a retired government official who lives in Flagstaff, Arizona, with her husband, recorded a story for National Public Radio in August 2006 about her aunt Mef. Here, she reminisces:

My aunt was Mary Elizabeth Ford, but I always called her "Mef"—an acronym from her initials. She was my father's only sibling, and she lived from 1910 to 1985. Mef was unmarried; a history teacher in Altoona, Pennsylvania, for her whole career; and an intrepid traveler, community volunteer, and pillar of the family through all her adult life.

Mef lived with our family for the first eight years of my life. Perhaps because of her close proximity, and the fact that I was her only niece, we developed a strong bond that lasted as long as she lived. My father died when I was seventeen, and she was the only link to his side of the family. Even now, twenty-plus years after her death, she is in my thoughts daily.

When Mef died in 1985, my mother and I cleaned out her house and discovered a cubbyhole inside a closet that was stuffed with paper bags containing nearly five hundred letters that I had written her over the years. The earliest was from 1954 when I was seven; the last was written just a few weeks before she died.

What a treasure! The best part of the discovery was realizing that she cared enough to save these letters. But almost as wonderful was reliving thirty years of my life, told in my own words. Over the years, Mef wrote me probably as many letters as I wrote her. Unfortunately, I saved only a few of hers.

One of my favorite letters to her was written in December 1962. It was several pages of my sob story about how the boy I liked couldn't take me to the Christmas dance because the band he played in had a job that night. I was devastated. Life was so unfair. I ended the letter by writing, "I'm so mad I could just cry. So there you have it—but, what are aunts for?"

Three days later, I had Mef's letter in reply. "Enclosed is a prompt answer to your question: What are aunts for? Your question reminded me of a quotation I copied years ago from Mrs. Miniver, *a novel by Jan Struther. 'I believe I am here to be a pattern and example to all aunts; to be a delight to girls and boys and a comfort to their parents; and to show that at least one daughter in every generation ought to remain unmarried and raise the profession of auntship to a fine art.' Thank you, Karen, for reminding me of it. I shall have to try again to live up to it."*

When I read through the letters, I realize how important she was in so many aspects of my life. Mef was a great role model as a strong, independent, unmarried woman. She had diabetes and gave herself a shot of insulin every day, but she didn't let that slow her down. She told me that anything worth doing is worth doing, even if you're not perfect at it. I still live by that motto. I've taken up hiking, sailing, and cross-country skiing. I've tried knitting, wood carving, and pottery. I'm expert at none of these, but delighted with all of them.

Mef was a friend, a mentor, a mother confessor, and a very savvy counselor. If cell phones had been around during Mef's life, her number would have been first on my "buddies list." I hope Mef knows that she more than lived up to her desire to raise the profession of auntship to a fine art.

BECOMING (AND REMAINING) A FAVORITE AUNT

Two different authors, separated widely in tone and times, offer universal pointers in the art of becoming and remaining a favorite aunt.

From Mary C. E. Wemyss, *The Professional Aunt* (1919):

As the children grow older the duties of the aunt become more arduous. For the benefit of schoolboy nephews with exeats [permission from school for a temporary absence], she must have an intimate acquaintance with the Hippodrome, any exhibition going, every place of instruction of a kind, or amusement. She must be thoroughly up in matinees, and know what plays are frightfully exciting, and she must have a nice taste in sweets. She need not necessarily eat them, it is perhaps better if she does not. But she must know where the very best are to be procured. She must never get tired. She must love driving in hansoms [horse-drawn cabs] and going on the top of buses. She must know where the white ones go, and where the red ones don't, although a mistake on her part is readily forgiven if it prolongs the drive without curtailing a performance of any kind. This requires great experience. She must set aside, moreover, a goodly sum every year for professional expenses.

And from "Meet Aunt Polly," a page on the sadly inactive Web site DearAuntPolly.com:

When Aunt Polly meets you, she doesn't care how you speak or what kind of grades you have. You are special to her, and she accepts you exactly as you are. Somehow, her acceptance inspires you to be yourself and to be your best. You dare to try different paths until you find your own. Along the way, you learn to respect the people and land and animals around you. If you have a problem, Aunt Polly has a story or a song to help you think about it. She can find something to laugh about in almost any situation, and when she can't she will comfort you in a deep way, underneath the tears.

Aunt Polly seems like a country aunt because she loves nature and the seasons and the quiet of a rural morning. She lives a slower pace and she always has time for tea. Her old house and rambling garden and the people in her town are very important to her. But Aunt Polly also keeps a bag packed under the stairs, just in case she has a last minute chance to travel. She has seen the desert and the ocean. She appreciates that there are whole separate worlds on every street. She loves to walk and watch the people, listen to their languages and learn their ways. Aunt Polly knows how to bring a little country to the city and a little city to the country and they both seem better for it when she is there.

In many ways, Aunt Polly seems young—always ready to play a game, hike a mountain, try something new. But she still believes in some of the old ways. Not just the old-fashioned milk-and-cookie ways, but the ways of the days gone by, when the elders held a place of honor by the fire and the children were proud to serve them. Sometimes, after sunset,

when Aunt Polly lights a candle and sits on the porch and tells stories, it seems like you are part of an ancient tribe and you want to dance and sing.

TEN GOLDEN RULES FOR AUNTS

1. Always talk up to nieces and nephews and assume they are slightly older than they are.
2. Find out what the nieces' and nephews' interests are, and listen to them without interruption.
3. Tell them about your own life, and what it's like to be you—these lessons may not register immediately, but they will sink in.
4. Presents don't have to be big or expensive, but they should be imaginative—and arrive on the right day.
5. For outings, follow the nieces' and nephews' enthusiasms, but don't fake yours. You may want to go and revisit your childhood at *The Nutcracker*—your nephews would probably prefer the latest blockbuster movie. Compromise by trying something new to both of you, and make it an adventure.
6. Get the nieces and nephews away from their parents, and see them on their own.
7. School is most children's favorite topic of conversation. Don't forget what their best subject is, or the name of their most loathed teacher.
8. Don't be too cozy. Aunts should expand the nieces' and nephews' range of experience.

9. Be fun, but don't try to be funny. Your idea of a joke will not be theirs, and all attempts to be "with it" will be instantly unmasked, leaving you branded as a phony.
10. Don't, please, remark how the children have grown since you last saw them. It's really irritating, remember?

A CONSTANT PRESENCE

Cathy, fifty-one, a pediatrician, and Karen, forty-nine, who oversees state government policies on families and children, of Silver Spring, Maryland, on being aunts to Johnny, nineteen, and Ellen, fifteen:

Cathy: We were always involved in their lives, but it intensified after their father, Kevin, died when they were only nine and six. At the time, we lived about an hour and a half away and saw them frequently. But after two years, we decided to switch jobs and move to be closer to them. We wanted to help Anne (Cathy's sister) raise them on a daily basis. So Anne bought a house and then we bought a house three blocks away. Our real estate agent and others sometimes express amazement that we're willing to do this. But we love the kids and want to be part of their lives.

Karen: For many reasons, we decided not to have our own children. So it has enhanced our lives to be close to Johnny and Ellen. They are my playmates. I'm more of the fun aunt, while they see Cathy as more of an extension of their own mother. I take them kayaking at sunrise or by moonlight. When we first moved we saw them four or five times a week, for dinner or the movies. Now that Johnny's away at college, one of us tries to leave work early when Anne has to work late, so one of us can keep Ellen company. We went to their soccer games and concerts and school plays. During the summers, we spend time with them at the family cabin in upstate New York.

Karen: I was touched when Johnny, many years ago, said that he wished we could get married. We are Ellen's godparents, which is unheard of in the Catholic Church, but their priest agreed. I was very close to Kevin and we talk about him a lot to the kids, about how he would have liked a particular movie that we've seen. I see a lot of him in them.

Cathy: We have certain traditions with the kids. Every year on their dad's birthday we go to dinner at a diner that he liked. We try to celebrate his life. We frame our own lives by their life stages. Johnny went to college this year; Ellen will be going soon. I would love to retire soon, but where we ultimately end up depends on where they are going to be. We don't ever want to be more than a few hours away from them. I love them like they're my own kids. We're not parents day to day. They are very close to Anne. Being aunts to them is a lot more fun.

THE GOLDEN RULES FOR NIECES AND NEPHEWS

1. Don't assume that you are the most important thing in your aunt's life.
2. A thank-you letter or message—by telephone or e-mail, if not by mail—is due for every gift or outing.
3. Remember your aunt's birthday, as she remembers yours.
4. Keep in mind that she's getting old, but don't remind her of it.
5. Tease her as much as you like, but don't call her "aunt" or "auntie" if she really doesn't like it.
6. Keep in touch.

TRAVELS WITH MY AUNT DEB

Dom Ashton, a student at Nottingham University in England, on his aunt Deborah:

Deb has always been a famous theatre and opera director, ever since I can remember. How would I describe her? Warm and exciting, friendly if she wants to be friendly, and bossy when she needs to be bossy. She attracts attention wherever she goes. She's not very domesticated; she doesn't cook, but she enjoys cleaning occasionally. She won't even pick up the phone unless she absolutely has to, but she's a very good texter and always replies very fast. She is very driven and very, very good fun.

My dad is a transport consultant, my mum a garden designer. We live in Hampshire, though I was brought up for the first five years of my life in Hong Kong and Wimbledon. I've got one brother, Lysander, who's five years older than I am.

Deb came out to see us when we lived in Hong Kong, but what I remember more vividly, from the age of about seven, is going to stay with her for a couple of nights, on my own, at her flat in Primrose Hill, something I've done regularly ever since. Now I can stay there even if she's not around.

We always have fun—when I was a kid, she used to let me eat ice cream in bed, and when I got a bit older we started going to lovely restaurants—sometimes posh ones, sometimes ordinary ones. She also took me to the theatre, often to shows that she'd directed.

She did similar things with my brother and my cousin Leo—he's a computer graphic designer. I don't think I'm her favorite, she's very evenhanded, but I'm the youngest, which I suppose has made a bit of a difference. She really did spoil us, but it wasn't anarchy. She certainly wouldn't let us get up to everything we wanted to, certainly not. We had a few rows when I was younger, but not major ones. Usually they were about trivial things, like when she asked me to ask a shop assistant something. For some reason, I didn't want to do that, and that could sometimes lead to arguments, particularly on our travels.

We talk about everything, especially matters relating to my family—I'm as open with her as I am with my mother. Unless I decided to join the army, she'd be very happy to support me in whatever I decide I might do.

Her work is very much part of our relationship, because she doesn't separate it from her life. We talk about it a lot, and I see virtually everything she does—the first thing, I think, was when I went to the Salzburg Festival when I was about ten, for her production of Coriolanus. *Then there was* Don Giovanni *at Glyndebourne, but I'm not such a big opera fan. Perhaps I love* *the plays she directs more—*Medea, *which I saw in New York, and* The PowerBook, *too. She's very nice about taking an interest in the plays I was in at school. When I was Horatio in* Hamlet, *she went through the text with me, which was a great help. It was a great pity she couldn't come to a performance.*

She's amazingly good at presents. This Christmas she gave me a couple of very fashionable T-shirts, but usually her gifts involve trips somewhere. She gave me Eurostar vouchers when the tunnel first opened, and we went to Paris together for three days—I was about eleven, and it was all so new that it was extra exciting. We did all the touristy things, like going to the Eiffel Tower and the Stade de France, and then we went out to dinner with Juliette Binoche. She often takes me along when she's meeting people. They're not business lunches exactly, but meetings with people she needs to stay in touch with for professional reasons.

We've been to Greece four times. She's got a friend, a theatre designer called Chloe, who has a house on Hydra, an island near Athens. This year we flew to Venice first and then took the ferry—it took thirty hours on a pretty grotty boat. We slept on the floor, but it was fun. Once we're in Greece, we tend to laze about in the sun reading, or we swim and snorkel, and there's always lots of talking and eating.

New York was another great trip. I hadn't been there before. We

went up the World Trade Center and stayed in a flashy hotel called the Hudson, had dinner at the River Café, and at my request went to see The Rocky Horror Show.

Perhaps the best birthday present was being an extra in her film The Last September. *I went over to Ireland for five days of the shooting. My finest moment is when you can see me running in front of Maggie Smith at a garden party. I am in the background in about five other scenes—a bit of favoritism, I guess! My brother, Lysander, didn't get to be in the film, but instead Deb flew him out to New York to be her companion at the Tony Awards, when she was nominated for* Medea.

Deb and my mum were close when they were children—there's a four-year age gap between them, my mother being the elder. My relationship to Deb is very different from the one I had with my mother—she's got the harder day-to-day job. I see Deb when it's a special occasion like a birthday or we do lovely things together.

She has taught me some important lessons of life. Her people skills are brilliant—the way she can get on with people, like waiters in restaurants, is amazing. The other day we got a free panettone in a restaurant in Primrose Hill because of the way she was joking with the waiters. She has also shown me how to get something done when it needs to be done.

I have another blood aunt. She's my father's sister, called Philida. She's in her sixties—she's really extremely nice, but basically a family person. She leads a different life from Deb's, and we tend to meet up with her at family get-togethers, which Deb can't always make. But as Philida has her own children, I've spent much less one-on-one time with her. And I suppose that's what it comes down to: One main reason that Deb's relationship with her nephews is so unique and exciting is that she hasn't got any children of her own.

EPILOGUE

Aunt Janet

At the funeral, the vicar gathered us around a raw square hole in the ground and asked if anyone wanted to place Janet's casket of ashes in the grave. I had loved my aunt deeply, and I owed her much. Family seniority also required me to volunteer, but my nerves paralyzed me and I stood rooted to the spot. My sister, braver and wiser than I am, stepped forward without any fuss and laid my aunt to rest. I don't know how she managed—even in the crematorium, I had come close to abject blubbering, squeezing my eyes shut when that dismally theatrical curtain was drawn across the plinth and the organ oozed out its pieties. Farewell, godspeed, most auntly of aunts.

Hers was not a dramatic existence, nor her story a particularly complex one, but it resonates with something George Eliot writes in *Middlemarch:* "If we had a keen vision and feeling of all ordinary human life, it would be like hearing the grass grow and the squirrel's heart beat, and we should die of that roar which lies on the other side of silence."

Gentle, patient, tolerant, loyal, watchful over those she loved, and in her latter years increasingly batty and infuriating, my aunt Janet had died at the ripe age of eighty-five, after an "ordinary human life" that rounded off with four miserable months in hospitals and convalescent homes. Her terminal condition had been variously diagnosed—heart trouble, a stroke, slow cancer—but my guess is that she simply faded away from the lack of any compelling reason to continue. She was never much of a fighter, and on the last occasion my sister and I saw her, we realized that she was quite calmly dying—she said as much several times, without concern, accepting it as self-evident.

I like to think she felt complete. She had fallen into a coma almost immediately after she had rallied enough to be taken gingerly out of the hospital for lunch. In a quiet country pub on a warm summer's afternoon, she sipped a glass of wine and swallowed a few mouthfuls of food, taking doddering pleasure in her surroundings and the company of her family.

A few days later, she went. Appropriately for someone so auntly, her deathbed was attended by her niece, my cousin, who reported that she rose up and smiled with something like joy before her head fell back on the pillow and she passed away—where to, I would like to know. My mother, her sister, to whom she was closely if imperfectly attuned, was later visited several times in the night by an inexplicable cool breeze that blew softly about her head and then evanesced. We know that this is Janet's spirit, drifting back in her unassertive way from the other side to let us know that she is at peace. If this sounds maudlin, I don't care; it's what we felt.

After the casket had been buried, we straggled back to her modest cottage for a wake. Aunt Janet had many friends in the Suffolk village in which she had lived for thirty years, and the tone of the proceedings was warm yet unsentimental. Two stout elderly ladies flirted coyly with the vicar, who got drunk, and a retired naval commander droned on about the decline of our armed forces. Eventually, when the bottles were empty, the mourners departed, most of them taking a token keepsake with them. We cleared up and sat numbly in the silence.

The next morning, my sister and I, her executors, opened the box containing her papers. A cursory rummage made it clear that despite the austerity of her outward circumstances, she had squirreled away a considerable amount of money, the great bulk of it bequeathed to her nephews and nieces. At that point, I was much more thrilled about something else: In an envelope addressed to me, I found a lovingly preserved program for the Aldeburgh Festival 1953, which she had visited. Music being my great passion, it was the most beautiful and auntly gift I could have imagined—a reminder of our bond, and the embodiment of many long conversations about Britten and E. M. Forster and string quartets and the theater and what life had been like in those grim yet optimistic days of postwar reconstruction.

The next morning, we locked up the cottage and left it without regret. It was a bleak little place, in the middle of a sprawling yet isolated village of no palpable charm. Aunt Janet was not puritanical, but she had no sensitivity to personal comforts or interest in material possessions. More out of force of habit than pleasure, she drank whiskey and smoked steadily: perhaps these practices numbed her to the penitential nature of her surroundings. There were no radiators, and the storage heaters were so tepidly ineffectual you wondered why they bothered. Hot water came dribbling reluctantly out of an Ascot boiler above the sink. The furniture was stolidly Victorian. Sideboards contained stacks of useless inherited cut class, crockery, and cutlery; shelves and mantelpieces were covered with knickknacks that provided neither ornament nor function. Nicotine-tinged walls were hung with pastoral scenes and family photographs. The bathroom was freezing, a crossroads for drafts and not a place to linger in a state of undress. A Dyson vacuum cleaner, standing in the hallway as if not yet feeling quite at home, struck an almost shockingly modern note.

Her clothes—well, we took them all to the charity shop. Most poignantly, by her bed, on a white plastic chest of drawers, sat the lifelines: blister packs and bottles of pills, a telephone, a reading light, paper tissues, and a Bible, with a bookmark in Ecclesiastes 7—"A good name is better than precious ointment." In her later years, she had become a communicant member of the Church of England, but my guess is that she clung to Christianity by her fingernails.

She had a good name, however, being truly moral—quite simply, she lived by her values: those long-lost Anglican, English home-front values relating to tactful honesty, mind-your-own-business neighborliness, good humor, self-respect, and emotional continence. She saw right and wrong clearly, balancing pity and sympathy with distaste and disgust. Her principles were firm without being rigid. "I have no time for such nonsense" was one of her favorite phrases, applied with equal dismissiveness to the bleeding-heart sentimentality of

Tony Blair and the Princess of Wales as to the hanging-and-flogging brigade.

Although I never heard her make overtly harsh judgments of individuals, her silences left one in no doubt as to what she thought. If something she deplored appeared on the television—*The Vicar of Dibley,* for example—a down-the-nose look of disdainful hauteur would set in, and very chilling it was, too. Once I took her to the ballet at Covent Garden—I thought naively that she would love the spectacle and grandeur of it all, but it was soon evident that she was quite unimpressed. She was similarly indifferent to lunch at my club and the sight of a minor television celebrity showing off at the next table. I used to work for a glossy magazine and thought it great fun. Without her ever saying a word, I was made stingingly aware that she despised my involvement in such extravagant, snobbish frippery, regarding it as unworthy of her family's name, the honor of which she protected like a lion.

Books that I published were therefore greeted with more respect, as worthy contributions to the ancestral annals, but she never gushed her praise. I was only doing what I had a duty to do, given my privileged circumstances, and her letters in response to the autographed copies I always sent her, though warm and encouraging and invariably bearing evidence of close reading, were also faintly chastening: This is all very well, she implied, but you could still do better. What she enjoyed seizing on was some minor detail—mention of a name or place—that fit the jigsaw of her own experience and memory. For example: "On page 143, you mention the village of Mickleham Parva. This rang a bell. I remember your grandfather visiting this place sometime before the war, where an old school friend of his was the Baptist minister. I think his name was Ernest Corrie."

Does all this make her sound humorless, solemn? Well, she wasn't, not in the least. She had a ready sense of the ridiculous, and her tendency to trivial chatter and rambling reminiscence infuriated her sister, my mother, an altogether more focused and motivated personality. One whiskey over her daily double and she would deliquesce into cascades of giggling: She adored stories of gaffes and misunderstandings, minor contretemps and small discomfitures and embarrassments. So, solemn, no; serious, yes.

Her life had not been outwardly eventful. Born into a solidly middle-class Oxfordshire environment in the early 1920s, she did well at school and just before the war went on to become—as she was always proud to inform you—the youngest-ever secretary at the Ministry of Works. It was a job she kept until

VE Day, when she joined a smart real estate agency. Her aspirations were limited to earning a seemly nine-to-five living—she expected nothing of her job, and didn't seem to mind that it entirely failed to stretch her good mind: What she really wanted was a man, a husband, a nest of security. But social timidity was her enemy here: She was reluctant to take any sort of initiative, and spent most of her evenings in London trailing in the wake of her more dashingly attractive younger sister, my mother, with whom she shared a room in a hostel for young ladies in Paddington. Anyone my mother fended off was passed to Janet, who sat there, like a dog at a dinner table, waiting for scraps.

In 1948, she married a surveyor, Clive Whittle—a friend of an ex-boyfriend of my mother's—and went to live in Wymondham in Norfolk. Her family was grim-faced about the match, aware that Janet didn't love the man. But she was without illusions: In those days, a respectable middle-class girl needed a husband, and in the aftermath of war they were not so easy to find. She would get on with him and make the most of it. For Janet, reaching beyond that would have taken a measure of heroism that she lacked.

Wymondham did not provide an auspicious start. Clive Whittle's home was the large and dank Victorian pile off the high street in which he'd been brought up. In an upstairs flat lived his mother—a rather sinister, twisted old woman who clung to her son with fervor and must have resented Janet's intrusion. In corridors, like figures in a Daphne du Maurier melodrama, the two women would pass without a glance, as if the other did not exist, and I can't recall them ever eating at the same table, even on holidays. I cannot imagine what the point of schism could have been—perhaps Mrs. Whittle's eternally stinking tomcat—but one felt that something had been said in a Homeric confrontation that could never be forgotten or forgiven.

Janet made some friends, however, and took to her wifely duties in a quiet country town. It could have been worse, one supposes. Any cruelty, any hatred was buried and silent. She was not a prisoner, there were diversions, and nearby Norwich with its antiquities and teashops was pleasant. She sat on committees, prompted for the amateur dramatic society, and eventually became a justice of the peace. She also read voraciously but critically, and greatly encouraged me in my own nascent bookishness. It was she who introduced me to Robert Louis Stevenson, for instance—I can vividly remember her whetting my appetite for *Kidnapped*, where my alter ego David Balfour grappled with miserly Uncle Ebenezer before running off with that noblest of head boys Alan Breck. We liked a little

Shakespeare, too, reciting "When shall we three meet again" in weird-sister voices, the murder of Julius Caesar, Malvolio's crossgarters, Pyramus and Thisbe, Prospero and Ariel.

One year she gave me *Northanger Abbey* for Christmas—I still have the copy, Wm. Collins and Sons the publishers. An odd choice, you might think, but actually one that showed exquisite auntly acumen and launched me on a lifetime's admiration of the matchless artistry and intelligence of another excellent English aunt with no time for nonsense, Jane Austen.

We visited Aunt Janet for a few days every year. The house in Wymondham gave me the creeps, in a thrilling way. Its warrens of sculleries, pantries, attics, and back staircases were all filled with the distinctive smell of old Mrs. Whittle's tomcat (or maybe of old Mrs. Whittle herself), and presented endless possibilities for hiding and seeking and fantasies of ghosts and treasures and secret passages.

Whenever we arrived, Aunt Janet presented us with a special tea—cucumber sandwiches, cupcakes, chocolate fingers, a Victoria sponge cake, and a jug of iced Day-Glo orange barley water—served at the dining room table, covered with the best linen cloth. After this welcoming spread, which seemed to have been produced at enormous effort, the refreshments became dismally spartan: There was a peculiarly depressing sort of

anonymous meat fricassee (mutton?) in a thick white sauce that was her standby, a greasy fried breakfast, and a rancid bread-and-butter pudding the thought of which makes me retch even now. (Food she always regarded as a necessity, a box of Milk Tray chocolates being her only sensual indulgence.)

There would be jaunts in the car to beauty spots, beaches, caves, and stately homes, but a lot of the time I simply sat opposite Aunt Janet in short gray trousers and told her everything I knew and everything that had happened to me since we had last met. God knows how she endured it, but she did, remembering the names of farcically fat boys in my class, the notable marks I had received in exams, the false teeth and gammy leg of war veteran Mr. Mee (scripture), the unjust punishments meted out by cruel young Mr. Tanner (history), the ludicrous lisp of Mrs. Parrinder (French), favorite Beatles tracks, my feats of ingenuity in the assembly of airplane kits and mechanical models. She listened, as it were, to the whole story of me, registering the nuances and refraining from judgments. I think that the realization that someone outside my immediate family circle could see me so clearly and see me whole gave me a valuable emotional confidence and a first lesson in the pleasure of intimacy—an auntly gift.

Meanwhile, she was desperately unhappy with Clive Whittle, though at the time I had no particular sense of this and he always seemed nice enough—a plump, affable film buff, with an intriguingly large hairy mole on his neck. After seventeen years, their marriage was annulled on the grounds of nonconsummation. I do not know the reasons for this, nor do I wish to speculate.

But she had fallen in love—at what stage, I am again unaware—with another Clive, Clive Hewson. He was a headmaster, divorced with three adult children, and a prominent figure in Wymondham. I know now that it was a long time brewing. One day, she unexpectedly came to stay with us. I came home from school, and there she was, unanticipated, weeding furiously in our tangled garden (she was good with flowers). She seemed distraught and her hands shook—what can she have been like when we were not there to inhibit her?

There was so much I wanted to tell her—my victory in the backstroke, a play about a shipwreck that I had written with Gibbs, the glory of the Beach Boys' surfing safari—but my mother implied that I should lay off. I was eleven, it was 1966, and there were things I did not understand. The fact was this: She had left Clive Whittle, and was going to live somewhere else with Clive Hewson. A large bunch of red roses was delivered. I saw the accompanying card, which read "To my beloved wife, please come home." She did not do so. Given her essential passivity and four-square morality, the decision to wrench herself away from Clive Whittle must have cost her enormous spiritual effort.

She and Clive Hewson, universally known on account of his rotundity as Pots, moved to Clanbury in Suffolk. After the annulment came through, they were married. It was too late for children, but Pots had three of his own, and she made as good a stepmother as she did an aunt. Pots taught at a grammar school; she worked part-time in a solicitor's office. In a variety of stately but unreliable old cars, they traveled over Europe, ran the film club, built a group of friends, tended a garden far prettier than their house, and made a decent, modest, righteous new life for themselves.

My mother was painfully divorced and needed to work. Unlike Janet, she was ambitious, talented, and sophisticated, and she made a success in the then new and glamorous profession of public relations. Her jobs often required her to travel abroad, and when our au pair girls could not be expected to cope with her more extended absences, Janet was called upon. She came reluctantly, I feel, being a creature who disliked disruption and responsibility.

I vividly remember her arriving at the station, walking down the platform in her one good Jaeger coat, carrying a Revelation suitcase. (Why Revelation, I thought, what was there to reveal? When she died nearly forty years later, I found it in a cupboard. Lined with moldy pink satin and a vanity mirror, it evoked a Proustian rush of memories.) Without experience of children of her own, Janet had absolutely no idea how to discipline us in a regular manner, and cast-iron rules about bedtime and television watching crumbled into glorious anarchy. The food under this non-regime was awful, though. She would select a can from the pantry, empty its contents into a pan, and turn on the gas. After some perfunctory stirring, she would transfer a pile of warm mush onto a plate. For pudding, there was a pink thing called Instant Whip, deliciously concocted of flavorings and additives. I think my mother's kitchen made her nervous.

One of these visits became the source of some acrimony.

The moment my mother returned from New York, Janet was packed and ready to go—they literally met in the front hall. We children were banished upstairs, and we heard a lot of shouting, then even more ominous silences followed by the slamming of the front door. "She expected me to take her to the station," I heard my mother spit to a friend on the telephone later. "All she cared about was getting back in time for Pots's birthday. Bloody selfish, that's what she is."

Perhaps she was a bit. And so was my mother, and so was I. Jealousy of Pots entered into it. Although he was truly the nicest and most reasonable of men—a loyal but not dogmatic Labor supporter of the old school, who had served in Malaya during the war—he alienated Aunt Janet from me. Or so it felt:

I was no longer the number one man in her life. Possibly my lapse into a phase of dopey longhaired mumbling teenagerhood didn't endear me to her, either.

But she never missed a birthday (checks, of a periodically ascending sum) or Christmas (usually something she had knit), and she continued to chart each step of my wayward progress. We had our bond, our conversation, our jokes and stock of literary allusions—one of our favorites, employed as an expression of outrage, being Lady Catherine de Burgh's "Are the shades of Pemberley to be thus polluted?" in *Pride and Prejudice*—for some reason, I thought this uproariously amusing. The trouble was that I still wanted her to myself, but on my terms. After the Beach Boys had come noisier and darker enthusiasms into which she couldn't follow me. The eleven-year-old who had wanted to tell her everything became a sixteen-year-old who wanted his life kept secret.

She and Pots enjoyed fifteen years of as much happiness as one can expect on earth. Then Pots's heart weakened, and he became querulous and feeble and mercifully died quietly. Janet was stoical in widowhood—grateful, I think, to have had what she had—but something inside her shut down, and she was never quite the same person again. She took to the church via a route I couldn't fathom, and as she declined into old age, her horizons steadily narrowed. She had always been thin and stooping, but now rheumatoid arthritis crippled her hands and made her face ache, and she became tetchy. She didn't moan, and she hated to be a bother. Her defensiveness made it all worse—she craved help, but was too proud to accept it with good grace. Beneath it all was a core of adamantine stubbornness, as displayed in her refusal to take a taxi if there was even the remotest possibility of a bus—or a lift. I hate to think of all the discomfort she suffered in order to leave her nieces and nephews money they did not really want or need. A generational thing, my friends tell me.

The balance of our relationship altered. Although she was pleased when I dropped my ridiculous fantasies of going onstage and became a writer instead, there was nothing she could do now, and it was left to me to take the initiative. I now wish achingly that I had seen more of her in these last years, but the drive to Clanbury was a bugger and her cottage unutterably joyless, so we kept urging her to come up to London and stay at my mother's sunny and cushioned flat in Highgate. We felt guilty about this, but providing extended hospitality agitated and taxed her. Should she turn the heating up or down? If I liked Earl Grey tea, she could get some in, but she made do with PG Tips. Did I like pasta (or par-sta, as she called it)—something that only entered her culinary repertory late in life? Had I locked the car, was the bed comfortable? (It wasn't.) Was I bored? Did I want to use the telephone or the washing machine, because if so, just go ahead and don't even ask? Did I know how grateful she was that I was bothering with an infirm old lady like her? That was the question that made it all so much worse.

Everything she owned was wearing out, alongside her own decrepitude—hence my surprise when I discovered that radiant Dyson vacuum cleaner. The Christmas before she died, we struggled one last time to the theater—Pinero's *The Magistrate*, not very good—and then I took her to a little Italian place for some "parsta." It was a quietly affectionate evening, even though her grasp of detail was weakening, and I think that she would have secretly preferred to avoid the Sturm und Drang of an evening out in the West End—not least as we returned to St. James's Square to find that my humble car had been vandalized. "Why do they do it?" she asked more in sorrow than in anger. "What pleasure can it give them?"

Two months later, she fell and was taken to the hospital, suffering more from confusion than broken bones. Clearly there wasn't anything much that could be done, and all one could hope was that she was free of pain or distress. My mother telephoned her almost daily, but her response was always vague and noncommittal. The doctors shrugged politely—this was a case of nature taking its course, they rightly implied, and I'm glad they didn't attempt any violent reversal of her condition.

But visiting her was an ordeal: I worried that she would be so far gone that she wouldn't recognize me, and that would have been hard to bear. When I went into the ward and saw her sitting in a chair beside the bed, her expression glazed and her wizened frame clad in a faded nightgown that she must have bought in 1965, I feared the worst. On a table sat a filthy little mess of lunch that she had barely touched. She clutched my wrist as I sat down.

"Aunt Janet," I said. "You really should try to eat something."

"I can't, dear, it's not very nice."

"But you must eat something." She looked like a starved bird that had lost its feathers.

"So, what's the news?" she asked with an attempt at interest and the vestige of her sweet smile.

"Oh nothing much. I think Tony Blair is in a lot of trouble."

"I haven't read a newspaper for months," she replied faintly.

"I was going skiing next month, but I've got so much work on that I've had to cancel."

She stared at me benignly, and the purple papery arthritic claw that was once her hand pressed my wrist sympathetically. "Are the shades of Pemberley to be thus polluted?" she quavered, in a voice that attempted to suggest the pomposity of Lady Catherine de Burgh. It was hardly a relevant response to my skiing plight, but it didn't matter. I knew what she meant, as she had always known what it was that I meant. A week later, she died.

ACKNOWLEDGMENTS

Rupert Christiansen wrote the original British edition of this book, which has been edited and adapted for an American readership by Beth Brophy.

Rupert Christiansen is indebted to an enormous number of friends who have contributed aunts and ideas to this book. Notable among them are Angela Abdesallam, Juliet Annan, Michael Arditti, Dominic Ashton, Ariane Bankes, Henrietta Bredin, Hattie Dorment, Charles Duff, Flossie Joll, Jonathan Keates, Lauro Martines, Robert Maxtone-Graham, Ysenda Maxtone-Smith, Gerald Martin Moore, Gley Moreno, Caroline Muir, Virginia Nicholson, Nicky Normanby, Sam Organ, Angus Robb, Felicity Rubinstein, Miranda Seymour, Adam Sisman, Lucinda Stevens, Zoe Svendsen, Robert Turnbull, Deborah Warner, Giles Waterfield, Ann Webb, Katherine Whitehorn, and Cristina Zilkha. His gratitude to the staff at the British Library and London Library, and to Tim Berners-Lee, whose invention of the Internet has transformed the possibilities of researching a book such as this.

Special thanks to his inspirational agent, Caroline Dawnay; to his late mother, Kate Christiansen, who gave great encouragement at the outset; and to Candia McWilliam, whose sharp and sensitive eye saved me from solecisms. Claire Pamment, Rachel Sussman, and Henrietta Bredin helped most effectively with research. At Faber, his marvelous editor Belinda Matthews has been—in perfectly judged balance—a constant support and occasional goad.

Beth Brophy thanks the people who shared with her their personal experiences of being aunts, and Nate Gray at Twelve for his research assistance.

About TWELVE

TWELVE was established in August 2005 with the objective of publishing no more than one book per month. We strive to publish the singular book, by authors who have a unique perspective and compelling authority. Works that explain our culture; that illuminate, inspire, provoke, and entertain. We seek to establish communities of conversation surrounding our books. Talented authors deserve attention not only from publishers, but from readers as well. To sell the book is only the beginning of our mission. To build avid audiences of readers who are enriched by these works—that is our ultimate purpose.